SEEKING
PASSAGE

Post-Structuralism,
Pedagogy,
Ethics

SEEKING
PASSAGE

Post-Structuralism,
Pedagogy,
Ethics

REBECCA A. MARTUSEWICZ

Teachers College, Columbia University
New York and London

Published by Teachers College Press, 1234 Amsterdam Avenue, New York, NY
10027

Library of Congress Cataloging-in-Publication Data

Martusewicz, Rebecca A.
    Seeking passage ; post-structuralism, pedagogy, ethics / Rebecca A.
Martusewicz.
        p. cm.
    Includes bibliographical references and index.
    ISBN 0-8077-4025-X (cloth : alk. paper)—ISBN 0-8077-4024-1 (pbk. : alk. paper)
    1. Education—Philosophy.   2. Postmodernism and education.
    3. Poststructuralism.   4. Ethics—Study and teaching.   I. Title.
    LB41 .M339 2000
    370'.1—dc21   00-047983

ISBN 0-8077-4024-1 (paper)
ISBN 0-8077-4025-X (cloth)

Printed on acid-free paper
Manufactured in the United States of America

08 07 06 05 04 03 02 01   8 7 6 5 4 3 2 1

Contents

Dedication:

For My Mother and Father

This is a book about the creative power of difference and its relationship to ethics and education. I tell stories throughout this text about my life and about some of the people (and nonhuman creatures) in my life that have contributed to the way I think about education. My mother, my brother, my lovers, my grandmothers, my grandfather, my students, my teachers, my friends— even my childhood horses and my dogs—all figure prominently in the chapters that follow. I write about some of the ways their lives have intersected with mine to explore the relation between the proliferating force of difference and the need to bring to it the power of an ethical question as a means of making the world a better place.

As I look over these stories, I am struck by an important absence. I haven't said more than a word or two about my father, one of my most important teachers. Now, not unlike other kids and their parents, my dad and I had our difficulties when I was growing up, especially during adolescence. I can say that these difficulties, which were sometimes quite painful for both of us, probably had much to do with my demands to be thought of as a thinker and a knower in my own right in the face of my father's authority. He was always the one who "knew" in our family, and I got pretty fed up with the exclusion that position implied for the rest of us. Perhaps some part of me needed to avoid a direct reckoning with those difficulties here. Even so, the dynamics of that story, though unwritten, circulate throughout several chapters in this book and have certainly affected how I think about education, culture, and feminism in particular.

But there is a more important story that I have only very recently realized—too late, unfortunately, to be analyzed fully into a chapter for this book. I share it here both as a testimony to my father and as a way to set the stage for the other stories and analyses to come. Although I did not really recognize it before, it was from him that I first learned about the relation between difference and love, so important to an ethical orientation to the world. I trust he won't mind my putting this on the printed page.

My father is a survivor of polio. When he was a year and a half old, the affliction known then as infantile paralysis left one of his legs severely under-developed. As my mom tells it, they didn't know back then that exercise would help. He grew up wearing a brace connected to a shoe worn on that leg, and walked (never skated, or jumped, or ran like other kids) with a limp. Ah, you might say, I see: The story is that you learned what it was like to live with someone who is handicapped.

No. The story is that I grew up never thinking of my father as handi-capped, never even really thinking about this smaller leg much at all except to the degree that it was part of my father. If he ever resented or felt sadness about his not being able to do certain things, he never showed it to his chil-dren. Rather, he taught us to respect (and challenge in our own struggles to grow up as independent adults) who he is, small leg or not. Even now, at the age of 71, my father is still about as strong a person as you'd ever want to meet. He worked as a builder most of his life, and his work made him physi-cally very strong. I remember being lifted into the air as a "flying angel" well into my early years—his "good" leg planted in my stomach—and looking down at the muscles in his arms.

But what was most important to my brothers and sister and me was a different kind of strength. It was what he and my mother taught us about the relation between difference and strength of character, difference and cour-age, and difference and ethical value through their relationship to each other and daily life with us. In many ways, directly and indirectly, my siblings and I learned that difference did not mean inferior, that we could make impor-tant choices about how we defined and understood difference. My father's different leg created all kinds of opportunities to think differently and more openly about people's abilities, about "normalcy," about all kinds of possibil-ity. It certainly never seemed to prohibit our explorations of the world. We did all kinds of things together, tramped and traveled all across the United States, camping in the most beautiful country from the southwest to the north-east, picking blueberries, fishing for trout, and hunting sand dollars. And we saw my mother deeply in love with and committed to my father.

I remember a friend asking me once about my dad's leg. Staring back at her blankly, it took me a couple of seconds to register what she was referring to. Not that it was ever hidden from view or a forbidden subject. He *was* dif-ferent. He grew up differently from any of his children or any of his own peers, and who he was, was a direct result of this difference. We all knew it, and yet we all grew up knowing him, valuing him, and loving him as this powerful man, our father—never as our father, the polio victim.

Thinking about all this now, I am struck by how my own sense of social justice—specifically, the idea that we ought to learn to value people for what they *do* bring to society, not what we assume they cannot, and for all the vast diversity they bring to the mix of social life—was shaped by this relationship to my father and mother. I want to honor here all they taught me in their quiet, unerring insistence that he be that person to us.

Differences are all around us; they shape us, and we make sense of them. As I will try to unravel in this book, what we make of them together is what is of utmost importance to our collective and individual happiness, our survival, and the survival of other life on this planet. This is what my father taught me. It has taken me a long time to appreciate this so clearly, or consciously, no doubt a paradox born of the way he has lived his life and the particular lesson that provided me. I thank him for that lesson now, for its power in shaping the ideas that have made this book possible. And I thank my mother too, whose love and influences are much more visible in the stories that follow. This book is dedicated to them.

Yspilanti, MI
January 28, 2000

Acknowledgments

So many people have contributed their insights, support, and care to me in the process of writing and thinking about the ideas contained here, I hardly know where to begin to express my thanks. Deleuze says we always begin in the middle, so here goes.

I thank Eastern Michigan University for the Faculty Research Fellowship and Sabbatical Leave, which gave me the time I needed to pull this project together. I also thank the university for being a supportive and stimulating community more generally; over the past 12 years, I have learned a tremendous amount from Eastern's students, faculty, and staff. Without this intellectual inspiration and support, I may never have written this book.

Many friends, students, and colleagues have read and commented on pieces of this manuscript, but one person has been there from the beginning, reading and critiquing every draft of every proposal and every chapter. Besides being one of my dearest friends, Kate Mehuron is one of the smartest people I know, and without realizing it, one of my most important teachers. Her comments on my work over the years have made inestimable contributions to these ideas. I can't thank her enough for the time she has spent helping me to clarify my arguments and for the support and friendship she has offered.

With Kate, I belong to a Writers Group composed of faculty from across the disciplines at Eastern. I am very grateful to have had the benefit of their critical insights on my work along with the excellent conversation about writing in general. They are Laura George, Rhonda Kinney, Craig Dionne, Paul Leighton, and Kenneth Kidd.

Others also have read and commented and deserve mention for their help as well as their friendship. Maureen McCormack, Stuart Henry, Brian Domino, Sandra Spickard Prettyman, Randy Havens, Barbara Tarockoff, Clara Thiry, Matt Anton, Richard and Martha Brosio, and Will Cares have given me very useful feedback and the kind of support that only comes from those who really care.

Lynda Barry wrote to me in support of the Maybonne chapter, giving me the thrill of a lifetime. I thank her for creating Maybonne and Marlys, for her lovely comments on my work, and for that swatch of Maybonne's dress fabric. The gift of her response was a much needed boost at a critical moment.

Jacques Daignault was an important teacher during the early Bergamo years. His groundbreaking work within post-structuralism and curriculum theory along with his friendship gave me the courage to say what was in my heart and to stop writing for any other reason.

Cork Martusewicz was there through many early struggles with these ideas. I thank him for his unwavering support and patience during those years.

J. Beth Gould, my graduate assistant and right-hand woman, painstakingly combed the final drafts of the manuscript, giving me excellent editorial advice as well as intellectual support.

Randy Havens has been my closest ally and support through the final grueling stages of this project. Our conversations and his comments on the Earth, Ethics, and Education chapter, especially, have led to many new and important insights.

I also appreciate the careful reading and excellent editorial work of the editors at Teachers College Press who strengthened my words and thus the ideas in *Seeking Passage*. What good teachers you have been! But especially I thank Brian Ellerbeck who stuck with me over so many years of developing this book. I owe him my gratitude for seeing potential in these ideas and for patiently seeing *Seeking Passage* through the last stages.

Preface

Looking back over the essays that comprise this book, I see them as a kind of travelogue, tracking the journey of thinking about education that I've been doing for 10 years or better. It's been a journey in and out and between lots of questions, concepts, and concerns about what we might really mean when we use the word *education*. Specifically, what is the relation between ethics and education? How can we define that relation in our concern for more socially just ways of living?

What I've learned in this process is that education would not occur without this journey or, more specifically, without what occurs between our points of arrival and departure among the myriad islands of ideas and theories that try to explain life. Hence, the title of this book, *Seeking Passage*, notes the unpredictable and sometimes risky pathways between the questions, between the texts, between the events and decisions that make up our becoming educated.

The essays collected here reflect some of the points along my own particular pathway and are thus intentionally autobiographical. Collectively, they are my attempt to reconceptualize in a more universal way what education means. Each essay takes up a specific question from my life as a means of trying to understand and explain what I believe to be the important relationship between teaching and learning, and a more just world. Thus, this book is my first attempt at articulating a philosophy of education.

I do so by drawing upon post-structuralism, primarily the thought of a handful of contemporary French philosophers—Gilles Deleuze, Michel Serres, Jacques Derrida, Michel Foucault—whose work I see as providing important analyses of the generative, creative force that humans use to create meaning in the world, including knowledge, culture, identity, and thus, importantly, education. Many contemporary interpretations see these works as political doctrine, often viewed as nihilistic and thus dangerous. To reduce these works to such political consequences, however, is to miss their important analyses of the creative power resulting from social life. A broad, interdisciplinary body of work, post-structuralism offers a kind of physics of culture, a close examination of the invisible particles and forces that get put into motion when humans attempt to make sense of, and thus create meaning in the world.

Using this framework, I analyze the effects of pedagogy and the possibilities for social transformation generated there, but I argue that education is only possible when we apply a specific question of well-being to these possibilities. Pedagogy and all its unpredictable generative potential, plus ethics and the specific decision making that questions of survival and well-being demand, create education and the possibility for a more just world.

I am primarily interested in the power of education to provide passages toward better ways of living and surviving together on this Earth. This is a book committed to issues of social and ecological justice. Our unique histories and experiences are connected to social, historical, and economic structures and relations, and thus to the lives of other unique individuals. I use autobiography as a way of exploring these connections, moving back and forth from vignettes from my life to theories that look at these larger structures. The stories that I tell here, as well as the questions raised from those stories, are thus both unique and connected to the larger world, offering passages (not universal answers) to thinking about larger collective issues of suffering and survival.

Each essay may be read as a story with its own integrity or with a connection to the other essays; each presents a set of circumstances with a particular interest in education and justice. This book, then, does not require a linear reading and is not organized in any chronological fashion. Nevertheless, the arrangement of the essays is intentional, and I have woven a thread of coherency using the questions and concepts that have inspired their collection in a book.

This is not an introductory text. Students will need the guidance of good translators—teachers with some background in philosophy, critical theory, and post-structuralism. Several of the essays here were originally written for a very specific audience. They were presented at Bergamo, a conference attended by curriculum theorists of a generally radical persuasion with strong social theory and philosophy backgrounds, who were interested in issues surrounding the relation of education and social justice. That said, I have crafted each chapter for a more general audience, hoping that some of the ideas might make sense to practicing teachers enrolled in graduate classes in the philosophy of education, as well as to social theorists interested in what post-structuralism might mean for an understanding of education. Although education students may have to stretch to grapple with the concepts employed, social theorists may have to be patient while I retread territory already familiar. I hope that I have made a translation strong enough to help those just starting out to begin to create their own passages between this philosophy and their own interpretations and experiences, while piquing the interest of and perhaps initiating new directions for those already on the journey.

The first chapter, "Seeking Passage: Post-Structuralism, Pedagogy, Ethics," lays out the general theoretical framework employed throughout the rest of the text. It defines the primary concepts taken from post-structuralism and argues for their usefulness to a philosophy of education. This chapter also discusses why autobiographical method is useful to such an endeavor. Beyond a simply descriptive method, I analyze this form of writing as a kind of translation that produces a new text, always already different from the life of the author and thus part of the very creative, generative force discussed throughout the book.

Chapter 2, "Leaving Home," draws on cultural geography, post-structuralism, and theories of translation to look at our relation to place and to space, analyzing the experience of leaving home as a metaphor for pedagogy as well as describing the kind of detachments (from what is familiar, comfortable, secure) necessary to becoming educated. Chapter 3, "Choreography and Curriculum Theory: Search for a Passage," explores my work as a choreographer for young figure skaters. I use French philosopher Gilles Deleuze's theory of repetition and difference, translating how repetition and difference work as the creative force in dance, pedagogy, and curriculum theory. In this chapter the relation between the play of difference and the need to judge introduces the question of ethics as it frames my definition of education.

This book also seeks to understand some of the cultural, psychological, and political forces that affect or even impede the generative pedagogical process and the questions we might bring to it in becoming educated. In Chapter 4, "Say Me to Me: Desire and Education," I recall my desire since childhood to be a scholar, to seek the "truth" through questions. Remembering my childhood excitement at the discovery that answers to questions lead to more questions and more answers in an indefinite series, I analyze in this essay how attention to this joyous desire for the truth and its power to produce new thought is essential to education. I then turn to an analysis of ways that this open, indefinite process can be shut down by another interfering desire— the desire for recognition and status (from mentors, peers, colleagues, parents, and so forth). I argue that too often our desire for power overcomes the will to truth, impeding the generative effects of pedagogy. Other chapters also look at interferences with the generative possibilities. In Chapter 5, "Maybonne and Me: Gender, Desire, and Education in *My Perfect Life*," I take a different tack on the problem of desire. Here I weave together an analysis of *My Perfect Life* by cartoonist Lynda Barry with memories of my adolescence and a reading of feminist theories to analyze the problematic relation between desire, feminine and masculine identities, and education in the context of schooling.

Chapter 6, "Suffering and Social Justice: Teaching in the Passage" draws on Buddhist philosophy together with post-structuralist philosophy to look at the problem of suffering as that which underlies all ethical questioning. Here I analyze what we could mean by "teaching for social justice" by looking carefully at the relations among the generative force of pedagogy, suffering as a fundamental result of human attempts to make sense of the world, and our ability to critically and ethically choose how to live. Drawing upon a variety of Buddhist teachings and anarchist philosophy along with poststructuralism, I argue that while our questions will never be answered nor suffering done away with once and for all, teachers with their students must learn to open their hearts to the well-being of others. As Buddhists teach, our own happiness depends upon such awakening.

Chapter 7, "Earth, Ethics, and Education," links an analysis of pedagogy as a generative process with ecological theories that view human life and nature as inextricably linked. Although educators have begun to take up the critical issue of social justice and multicultural education, most theorists and teacher educators leave untouched the even more fundamental and certainly related question of education's significance to our earthly survival. Making a translation between Deleuze's notion of repetition and difference and the work of nineteenth-century anarchist philosopher Mikhail Bakunin, this chapter calls attention to the ethical significance of these ecological issues for teacher education. Does pedagogy, as a creative process offer any help in the dilemma that we face with Mother Earth? What is our ethical responsibility as educators in this crisis?

Writing these essays has been an important personal journey that will be relevant to others interested in the transformative power of education. Along the way, I have become conscious of an underlying spirituality that accompanies these ideas. This spirituality is not from any religious affiliation, but rather from a faith in the power of life, a desire to understand the powerful life forces that run through us and connect us to each other and the rest of the world; it also refers to a commitment to the alleviation of suffering through a particular view of education as born of a creative life force and as an ethical approach to living. In the essays collected here, I use language that expresses how I experience this generative force as it connects me sensually as well as intellectually to practices and effects that I describe as fundamentally pedagogical.

Many of the concepts and analyses that I make in this book gesture toward processes that connect us to larger life forces in the world, those complex relations that Buddhists refer to as *interbeing*. And while I am centrally concerned in this book with ethics, I do not find any universal ethical answers in those forces. Rather, I argue that using the power of interpretation and questions born of these differentiating forces, we have the responsibility and capacity to choose collectively those forms that will promote life, beauty, and well-being in our communities. How and whether we do so is always up in the air.

Introduction

The other day I walked into one of my undergraduate classes exhausted, grumpy, and really underprepared to deal with the material I had assigned my students to read. I had been reading their midterm essay exams. I felt somewhat disappointed at what was not in those essays, and I knew I could not just let it be. I told them that I was tired but we really needed to look again at some of the theories of social inequality we had been dealing with throughout the term. We began. I lectured (rather grudgingly since it is not something I am comfortable with, or usually do); they listened. I asked definitional questions; they worked at getting the answers "right." We were looking at the differences between deprivation theories of inequality and social reproduction theory, specifically at how poverty might be understood from these very different perspectives. They regurgitated William Ryan's (1976) argument that theories defining individuals as being genetically deficient or families as lacking the "correct" values essentially blamed the victims of inequality for their plight. We looked again at Jean Anyon's thesis (1981) that the practices, materials, and curriculum in schools actually function to reproduce social classes and thus the unequal social structure. Finally I said, "OK, now what does any of this have to do with what we might do in a classroom with students? Why should we care?"

All of a sudden the class ignited into a fiery and impassioned discussion! Questions flew around the room, and students responded to each other with clarity and energy. "If inequality is imbedded in the practices teachers use, then how should we be teaching?" "Inequality really comes down to some kids being valued differently than others; that means some kids suffer because of the attitudes of teachers, schools, and the larger society." "Yes, but blaming the teachers is also blaming the victim, isn't it?" "Wait a minute, aren't some families really to blame for how their kids act? Are parents suddenly off the hook?" "Shouldn't we be talking about more than just schools? What about the media, organized religion, . . . ?" "If we're going to talk about the ways kids are treated in schools, how about the ways that we're taught to treat animals or the environment? Talk about suffering!" "Well, the Bible says that . . ."

I sat there amazed while they took over. My heart was pounding, and I was aware of something welling up in my throat. Their questions were so poignant! They weren't just mimicking my point of view; we had never addressed many of their insights. I didn't even agree with all of their thoughts, nor did they all agree with each other, but oh, the thought that was created! Suddenly, seemingly from nowhere, what had started off as a daunting, depressing task of revisiting old turf turned into a blast of fresh air. They were *thinking*—and I was full with the joy of it. "Holy cow!" I thought. "Where did this come from? What had happened among these students and me to create such a wildly different set of responses?"

This book lays out a philososphy of education that begins with a close examination of the teaching-learning relation, that is, what happens or what gets made *between* teachers and learners in all kinds of different contexts. I examine the factors creating the generative force inherent in pedagogy and specific ways that this force can be kept alive or shut down. I analyze how, in the relation between teachers and learners, all possible kinds of ideas, beliefs, interpretatons, and meanings are generated because of the operation of a potent generative force that depends on difference as its fuel.

Further, I look at education as a relation that brings to bear the complicated play of ethics upon this generative pedagogical force. Thus, I define education in the essays presented here as something different from pedagogy. I argue that to become educated requires not only an attention to questions regarding the welfare of self and others but also a willingness to confront and shift one's own habits, practices, and beliefs for that purpose. While pedagogy offers the creative process necessary to generate the questions and all possible answers, education demands a willingness to judge, to choose between all possibilities for the well-being of one's self and community. Education must be framed by the decisive confrontation with issues of social and ecological justice.

Interbeing and Difference: Affirming Life

To get beneath those more academic introductory remarks, this is a book in which I try to understand myself, my own experiences as they are connected with others, with the faith that these experiences are at once singular and yet not unique to me. I begin from questions that arise out of my life, moments that connect me and are imbedded in larger cultural processes. I use these questions not as a means of universalizing my experiences but rather as a means of moving toward an analysis of a larger, more global generative force or spirit that is created among humans and between them and the larger living world. I am certain that looking closely at this generative spirit could teach us much about education.

Ever since I was a little girl—I really don't know when I was first conscious of this—I have carried with me a sense of the world, its forces, its life, that burns in my heart. I feel the world in my body. I make sense of this feeling as a joyful, affirmative movement of life forces that play on our bodies as we interact with and think about the world. Think, for example, of that feeling you get, the lump in your throat or the shivers down your spine, when you stand in the presence of something really awesome, something that touches you deeply. For me, it might be a beautiful forest, gently falling snow, and cooing wind coming through a stand of huge monarch pines; or it might be a group of undergraduates, voices rising in excitment as they begin working out ideas about how to teach in ways that are antiracist or antisexist. There's a charge in the air, and if we stop for just a moment, we might recognize it manifesting as a prickle on our skin or a sparkle in someone's eye.

As we attempt to make sense of it and respond to it, as we appreciate its beauty or respond to its suffering, the world comes to us not only intellectually, as an idea or concept, but also physically, sensually. Often for me, the simple act of trying to figure out answers to difficult or perplexing questions brings a rush of joy that fills me up and pushes me forward. French philosopher Michel Serres taps into this sensual life-giving experience, writing:

> If I had to name the dominant sentiment that is always with me, I would not hesitate a moment: joy, the immense, sparkling, indeed holy joy of having to think—a joy that is sometimes even serenity. (1995a, p. 42)

The world and the meaning we make of it plays on our bodies as an affirmative force. In this book I want to pay attention to that force, especially as it manifests itself in pedagogical relations. I begin, then, from the belief (generated in part from my own experience) that our sense of joy as well as our experiences of suffering are made between our thinking and a creative life force. To think about education is to consider carefully how this force works, to be mindful, as Vietnamese Buddhist Thich Nhat Hanh (1988, 1993) might say, of our *interbeing* with the larger life forces and nonhuman creatures of the world.

Since I cannot remember a time when I did not have language or the desire to express, the sense that we are part of a larger creative life force has always found its way into words, questions, or even other forms like dance when I skated, for example. In turn, the attempt to say something with words or with my body often generates bursts of laughter at the sheer joy of seeing and feeling the creative process that results. This is why I love to write and to teach in spite of the difficulties that accompany these activities. I feel intense love and peace in these moments.

I want to think about what interbeing and the meanings we make between us might teach us about education, about our willingness and ability
to alleviate suffering, to create new ideas for better, more just ways of living
together. What, in short, is the relation between this creative force made
between us and our future survival and well-being on this planet?

Throughout the book I will argue that this force runs through and is
generated within all kinds of differentiating spaces, including the space between self and other. It is this space, and our attempts to communicate across
it, that interests post-structuralist philosophers. Hence my interest in their
work.

As humans, we try to communicate, to think, to teach, to learn, and to
know across the space between ourselves and others, ourselves and the world.
The effects created through these attempts are made because of the *difference* between ourselves and the outside, hence the space between is a differentiating space. Social relations of all kinds are creative, or as post-structuralists
following Niestzche would say, they are *affirmative* because the space between us requires that we create meaning. Communication, as we shall see
in more detail in the next chapter, is never simply transmissive, but always
productive of meaning. Over the years, I have come to think about this generative process as definitively pedagogical.

My interest in this book is to look carefully at what happens in the passage between teachers and learners. What makes transformation possible even
while we set strict goals and define limits? I do not deny that goals, objectives, and a clear sense of purpose are all necessary to teaching. Teachers,
like writers, artists, or dancers, are in the business of communicating something to someone; they are also accountable for goals set by the state and their
local districts. I would never say that attention to outcomes is unimportant
or unnecessary. Rather, I will argue that there is a tension between what we
plan and what actually happens that is worth looking at carefully.

A Passage Beyond Critical Pedagogy

Teacher educators are undoubtedly familiar with the debate between ap-
proaches to teaching that emphasize transmission of information and those
that strive for transformation of the given social structures and relations. Traditionally, much research around the teaching-learning, or pedagogical, relationship focuses on the control and predictability of outcomes, emphasizing
efficiency in the organization and delivery of curriculum. In this technical-
rational approach, *curriculum* is defined as the formal content to be taught,
and *pedagogy* is conceived of primarily as the transmission of that content
from teacher to learner. The primary purpose of teaching in this view is, as

Ralph Tyler wrote, "to change patterns of student behavior through carefully defined objectives" (quoted in Kliebard, 1995, p. 188). Most of us are products of this approach to teaching and the associated organization of schooling. Indeed, it remains the dominant way of thinking about what it means to teach in the public school as well as the university.

Charging that this approach to teaching and learning functions to reproduce existing unequal social structures and hence unequal power relations, a second approach to pedagogy emerged. Against the above transmissive perspective, critical educational theorists have argued for pedagogy as a crucial process for social transformation. In this view, pedagogy is a process through which both individuals and groups of individuals (socioeconomic classes, ethnic or gendered groups, for example) contribute to the creation of culture and their own liberation. As pointed out by Kathleen Weiler, these theorists "focus on the ways in which both teachers and students in schools produce meaning and culture through their own resistance and their own individual and collective consciousness" (1988, p. 11). While my own work is clearly influenced by this general perspective, critics have pointed to some important problems in this theoretical approach to pedagogy (often referred to as critical or feminist pedagogy).

The most important critique of critical pedagogy from this third perspective has been that it simply substitutes one set of ideological objectives—and hence political outcomes—with another, creating and transmitting, as Jennifer Gore (1993) has pointed out, its own "regime of truth." Elizabeth Ellsworth's well-known essay "Why Doesn't This Feel Empowering" (1989) introduced us to students' experiences of "liberatory pedagogy" as too often fraught with authoritarianism and dogma. Hence, "truth" in this perspective as in the more traditional transmission approach is seen to be had by some (the teachers) and not by others (the students), and liberation is often seen as possible only when the students "get it."

In other words, although the desired outcomes may change to include the transformation of existing social structures, the primary definition of the pedagogical relationship continues to emphasize the use of specific objectives and outcomes (held and defined by the teacher) leading to desired changes in patterns of student behavior. How do we stay committed to emancipation and social justice without falling into such authoritarian traps? Part of the problem here is where one locates the potential for transformation. Is it in the content, attitudes, and beliefs held by the educator, in the resistance of the students to those beliefs, or in the creative relation developed between the students and the educator? Whether the goal is the reproduction of social structures or the transformation of those structures, if the "truth" is held to be a stable object, the basic understanding of pedagogy remains the same, and what comes to be defined as education is too often, in my view, indoctrination.

The focus on predictable outcomes as the primary interest or goal of good pedagogy ignores much that is created in that relation between teachers and students. In this book, I'd like to shift the focus to look at the generative forces created between teacher and learner while recognizing the tension created as a result of the need to teach something to someone. I am interested in what happens between teachers and learners in spite of the intentions that must be taken into account as we think about the relation between pedagogy and a better world.

Pedagogy as a Generative Force

While teaching is always an intentional act, pedagogical relations create effects that escape intention, and these effects are what open the door to different visions and to new thoughts about the world. The key to moving out of authoritarian frameworks in our search for more just ways of being is to recognize *the infinite operation of difference* resulting from our own attempts to think about the world.

Difference is a productive force that always comes to undermine the "truth" and certainty whether we want it to or not. Pedagogy is a creative, difference-producing relation, resulting from a space between self and other where a kind of translation takes place and something new gets made. Embracing this differential creative spirit is part of what it means to become educated. Several essays in this book return to moments in my own life when this creative spirit has been most present, to explore what it might teach us about education, especially as it is mediated by an ethical orientation to the world.

I am committed to the notion that as educators we must be engaged with others in questions about the kinds of communities we want to live in, the kinds of knowledge and experiences that are most worthwhile, and the kinds of people we want our students to become, even while we may never completely agree upon the answers to those questions. I am committed in particular to asking students to look carefully at suffering in whatever form it may present itself, as the ground zero of all our ethical decision making.

Throughout this book, it will be clear that I take strong ethical positions on a variety of issues including the politics of knowledge and schooling, the social construction of desire, and our relation and responsibility to the Earth, as well as to each other. The stands that I take on these issues are particular to my life history and are therefore in some sense singular; and yet, they have been created within a historical, cultural, and political context and so are also in some sense collectively experienced and meaningful. Far from a universal or *a priori* truth, they are created within a specific context.

This historical collective context is political, teeming with variety and thus with all kinds of interests and ideas. Therefore, if there is a teleology to my conception of the ethical, it is one developed socially and historically, not universally. I do not see the ethical positions that I take in this book as the only positions to be considered but rather as part of a number—perhaps an infinite number—of possible choices to be considered relative to questions of how we should live together. This wide range of possibilities are the result of the generative force of difference.

I am also very aware that my approach will appear contradictory to those who believe that the post-structuralist affirmation of difference and "the local" (or individual experiences and identities) is somehow opposed to or exclusive of a commitment to community, global politics, or an ethical way of life. Yet, I am certain that the positions taken in this book are only possible *because* of the differential processes that I describe as inherent to pedagogical relations. I do not use post-structuralism as a political model but rather as a way of analyzing the way culture, knowledge, and meanings of all kinds get made.

A commitment to difference does not mean that there is anything inherently good in such processes. Rather, differentiation is the source of *any* position, idea, or belief—terrorist, nihilist, liberatory, feminist, conservative, radical, and so forth. Yet, the attention to such processes is not exclusive of an interest in making personal and collective choices for a better world. While difference is precisely what makes democratic processes so unruly and difficult, what we face is not a matter of opposing differentiating forces to an ethical or moral position.

Rather than contradictory, I see specific political and ethical stands taken and the desire or impulse to do so (as well as indifference to such questions) as resulting from differentiating relations including, perhaps especially, those defined as pedagogical. I look for ways of demonstrating that *hope* for thinking about better ways of living is possible *precisely* because of the affirmative operation of difference. Again, by affirmative I mean that everything, all meaning, is possible because of this specific productive force.

The essays in this book are created with the help of writers and thinkers who also tune in to this affirmative process, seeking passage toward hope and joy, well-being and justice. I find the work of the so-called post-structuralists most useful for their attention to and explanations of the movement and play of creative forces in the world, whether it be in literary texts, sociopolitical relations, or ecosystems. And there are other voices—Buddhists and anarchists, poets and ecologists—whose sense of the world touches me for its sensitivity to questions of justice, suffering, and the creative force necessary to create passages to a better world. Thus, this book seeks connective passages between the ideas introduced by these theorists and questions gleaned from moments in my life to think about education.

Chapter 1

Seeking Passage

Post-Structuralism, Pedagogy, Ethics

In an effort to make sense with my students of how we come to accept and perpetuate ideas and behaviors that degrade some and value others, I often find myself telling them a story. I remember driving along in the car with a friend one day, early on in my graduate program. We were listening to the radio, and the DJ made some comment about women on welfare. It was sexist and clearly blamed their poverty on some assumed inherent flaw. I began to rant at the radio. "Aw, Beck," my friend said, "that's just the way it is. It's in their culture." Suddenly, I became wide awake to two intertwined processes: First, ideas and definitions about who we are in the world and who "others" are, are created and insidiously maintained in our day-to-day interactions and conversations. And second, we can interrupt such a naturalized process with important questions. "No way!" I shouted, "It's not the way it is! It's the way we allow it to be! We *make* it so!" That was a crystallizing moment in my commitment to education as a process by which we can shift our relationship to the world in order to promote well-being and happiness.

To think about education, to pursue it, is to be interested in the transformation of "the ways things are" into more just and healthy relations, structures, and ways of thinking and being. It is to analyze and ultimately refuse the rationalizations that assert natural hierarchies of value in which some people get to live fuller, richer, safer lives by virtue of historically constructed and embedded ideas of who they are. It is to be interested fundamentally in the alleviation of suffering and the creation of well-being in the world.

This pursuit requires attention to two simultaneous and seemingly contradictory processes: (1) the proliferation of difference in our understandings and inventions of how the world works; and (2) the assertion of an ethical imperative, that is, the question of how we should live together on this earth given our invention of all the possible forms. Becoming educated requires that we understand how we have created our relation to the world in which we live. Moreover, it requires that we invent different forms while choosing those that are most beneficial to our communities and to the larger world. To do

8

this means that we must become courageous nomads, seekers of heretofore uncharted passages.

This chapter introduces the theoretical foundation for such a definition of education. In a serious consideration of how invention is possible and thus what constitutes the generative force of pedagogy, I look carefully at analyses of difference as the fuel of that force. Then, defining education as something different from the teaching-learning relation, I consider how ethics might be applied to these analyses. I begin with the work of French philosopher of science Michel Serres.

Multiplicity and Passage

> The passage is rare and narrow. . . . From the sciences of man to the exact sciences, or inversely, the path does not cross a homogeneous and empty space. Usually the passage is closed, either by land masses or by ice floes, or perhaps by the fact that one becomes lost. And if the passage is open, it follows a path that is difficult to gauge.
>
> (Serres, 1982, p. xi)

The work of Michel Serres has been inspirational to me, not only for its breadth and depth but also for the courage Serres has for navigating difficult passages between seemingly unrelated and unrelatable terms or bodies of knowledge. For Serres, the natural sciences, mathematics, literature, mythology, and philosophy have been islands of thought that when linked inform us of the political and cultural landscape that is human life. Emphasizing chaos, with its complexity and multiplicity, Serres argues against ways of thinking that present the world as organized by universalized patterns or structures. Such patterns are simply made by our attempts to make sense out of the chaos.

> The real is not cut up into regular patterns; it is sporadic, spaces and times with straits and passes. . . . I am looking for the passage among these complicated cuttings. I believe I see that the state of things consists of islands sown in archipelagos on the noisy, poorly-understood disorder of the sea . . . the emergence of sporadic rationalities that are not evidently linked. Passages exist I know . . . but I cannot generalize, obstructions are manifest and counter-examples exist. (1982, p. xxi)

Serres argues for attempting to "see on a large scale, to be in possession of a multiple and sometimes connected intellection" (p. xiii). Against the history of Western philosophy, he argues that there are no universal models to guide us toward understanding. There are only diverse and multiple islands of possible thought and meaning in a noisy sea, whose connections must be searched for or invented, and may exist or may not, but must not be assumed.

This means that the answers to the question, how are we to live, are not present in some undiscovered universal truth. The answers to this question lie in our ability to think in multiple ways and to seek connections, creating links between perhaps heretofore disconnected ideas. This is a process of creation made between us as we think together, rather than discovered outside. The implications of this way of understanding thought are important for how we think of education since it assumes that hope for a better world is located in our ability to invent it.

To search for passage is not only to look for connections in the chaos as the pursuit of understanding but also, as part of the creative and affirmative process of thinking, to seek peace and joy among disorder and difference: to seek our connection to interbeing through thinking. For while there may be no underlying orderly global pattern or model, the forces of difference and multiplicity that thinking and creativity bring open the possibility of connection. What we have is the ability (though not always the freedom) to think toward more ethical ways of being in the world, but this means looking for what blocks these possibilities as well as for passages toward understanding and respecting each other. For Buddhists, this means that we must have compassion, to open ourselves to others' suffering in order to alleviate it and thereby create happiness for ourselves.

Such opening requires the constant reinvention of thought and, consequently, of the freedom of thought. For educators interested in social justice, this requires that we both understand the potential in our relations with students for infinite creation of new ideas, encouraging multiplicity in their ideas, and accept the responsibility to teach them to bring to bear important questions of well-being on these ideas. It requires that we learn with our students how to choose carefully and critically from among the possibilities generated in the chaotic multiple pedagogical process. It also requires that we recognize those forms, behaviors, and processes that might shut down or block these creative possibilities.

"Unfortunately," Serres writes, "thought is usually only found constrained and forced, in a context rigid with impossibilities" (1995a, p. 43). Thus, he encourages us to challenge and replace models of thinking or of teaching that reify and exclude, with the hope (and uncertainty) of difference and multiplicity. "One must resolutely open a new epistemological spectrum and read the colors that our prejudices had previously erased" (1982, p. xiv). Passages beyond those prejudices, beyond domination and suffering, exist; we must learn to seek them.

I adopt this notion of the passage as a metaphor for my own work and as a way of thinking about pedagogy as a creative, unpredictable, and often jarring journey between life experiences and knowledge forms. "Seeking passage" refers to the experience that teachers and students go through as they seek answers to their questions, as well as to my own project of thinking about the teaching and learning relation.

My work is decidedly autobiographical, not as a narcissistic or nostalgic practice but rather as a means of seeking pathways between questions that arise from the specificity—or, as Serres would say, the singularity—of my own life history and bodily experience of the world and larger cultural processes from which my experiences emerge and are shaped. As nineteenth-century anarchist philosopher Mikhail Bakunin might say, this life of mine is part and parcel of a larger set of cultural transformations, and so offers a jumping-off place to begin to look at these larger processes. In this way, *Seeking Passage* explores some moments in my own history, those parts of the text of my life that help me to make sense of or ask questions of the larger world, in particular what we might mean by the concept of education.

Moving between storied moments or passages in my life and the ideas offered by post-structuralism, I create pathways for thinking about the relationships among pedagogy, ethics, and education.

Experience, Language, Difference:
The Movement of Meaning

Post-structuralism, a broad, multidimensional, and far from unified set of writings, examines the relation between language and its use to understand social and personal experience. All experience and knowledge in this view must be understood as filtered, meaningful only through the symbolic order—language and culture. Nothing may be known of experience before language since it is language that mediates between the world and our knowledge of it. Thus, the search for the origin of meaning, the historic quest of philosophy and science, is ultimately caught in the paradox of representation. What we know is what we can say about the world, and what we say is nothing more or less than a distanced re-presentation predicated upon difference; it is never the world itself. "In the beginning is substitution" (Serres, 1997, p. 62).

One of the most important contributions to contemporary philosophy made by post-structuralists is their particular notion of text. Post-structuralists define *text* as any set of symbolic objects (not just words) through which we try to communicate something and through which we thus create meaning. Classrooms, movies, books, and clothing, for example, all function "textually."

Moreover, they do so because not only do we create them, we also "read" them. This means that texts are never simply the objective result of an author's intention, but include those excess meanings manifested in our personal and collective interpretations of them.

Meaning is not just inherent in the text, or given by the author, but rather created by the meanings and assumptions brought to it by the reader. We bring our histories, our desires, our politics, and our values to a particular text or situation ("con*text*") to make sense of it. Each time we read, we are also in the process of creating an interpretation and hence meaning in the text. Thus, meaning is fluid and an author can never predict what meaning a particular text will have for her readers. Even though she may work hard to get a particular feeling or theme across, there are always already many more possible interpretations than those which the author can control. As Michel Foucault puts it,

> Interpretation can never be brought to an end, simply because there is nothing to interpret. There is nothing *primary* to be interpreted, since fundamentally, everything is already interpretation; every sign is, in itself, not the thing susceptible to interpretation but the interpretation of other signs. (quoted in Descombes, 1980, p. 117; emphasis added)

Because of our inescapable relation to a symbolic system as members of culture, there is always an "originary difference" at play in the process of knowing. That is, what we say about the world is always different from the world itself, and there is always this differential space between the world and our representation or knowledge of it.

From the French verb *differer*, meaning both "to differ" and "to defer," Jacques Derrida creates the concept *differánce*. The double meaning of *differánce* is important. It denotes the process of differentiation at play in the production of meaning (and thus of knowledge) as well as the movement of deferred meaning, or other possible interpretations. With this deliberately ambiguous term, Derrida strives to undermine the notion that meaning, knowledge, and therefore even human subjectivity are static, stable, or predictable entities. Rather, meaning is constituted of the infinite play and movement in the relation between signs. It is never stable because of the differences generated in the spaces between signifying entities—signs, words, gestures. One set of meanings may immediately be reread and thus forms a "supplement" to the last, in a long chain of transformative interpretive history. Human history, hence culture, is the result of the transformative effects created by this moving process of supplementarity.

The supplemental movement of meaning and its effects cannot be seen or touched or caught. It is invisible; it does not "exist," and yet it plays on the body. As Deleuze (1990) would say, its effects "subsist." Thus, the movement and play of meaning is not an exclusively intellectual experience, disconnected from what we feel sensually.

Differences created among words and gestures touch us, rising up in our throats or sending shivers down our spines. When I talk about a sense of movement that plays on my body, I mean that the unpredictability and excess created in my attempts to say something about or understand someone else's interpretation of the world often create intense unexpected and emotion-provoking meaning that my body feels. Thinking engages us with the world sensually.

Noise, Excess, and the Excluded Third

When we think about ourselves in the world, we quickly discover that there is more to say than our words can capture. Serres (1982) writes about the "beautiful noise" or the "excess empirical" of every text and every claim to knowledge, in the spaces of meaning that escape the capture of representation. For Serres, the world, in all its complexity, is composed of noise. It is a human endeavor to try to organize the chaos into patterns and regulated forms or to search for passages between the islands. Every reading and every conversation or dialogue, he tells us, attests to the existence of this excess.

When we speak to someone, we work hard to try to communicate something, choosing to say this instead of that, using one nuance or tone rather than another. We are always making some choices and excluding others. The person to whom we speak must also strive to receive the message because there is always the potential of "misinterpretation," or excess meaning interfering with the conversation. To have a successful conversation, therefore, two people try to exclude (whether consciously or not) the static or noise from the conversation. "In a certain sense," writes Serres, "they struggle together against the demon, against the third man" (1982, p. 67).

Serres's analysis of the invisible "third man" reminds us of the paradoxical experience involved in all attempts to communicate with each other and the problematics involved in all attempts to dialogue. That is, while it is human to search for connection and common experience with others, our use of language (or symbolic systems in general) to do so is always productive of interferences with that process. The search for identity is constantly challenged by the generation of differences, and this paradox is at the heart of the democratic process.

Much of what we do as teachers, as students, and as theorists occurs in or as conversation. Yet, no matter how hard we try, we never succeed in excluding this noisy third: Other possible interpretations and meanings are always there waiting to interfere, and the "excess empirical" (the force of potential meaning) that is part of the creative life force of the world is always at play. Our "struggle" to find our way through the chaos via our readings, our interpretations, and our translations is at the heart of the creative process that is necessary to open possibilities for a better world.

Repetition and Difference: A Paradox of Sense

Offering an important development of paradoxical thinking, Gilles Deleuze, another contemporary French philosopher, focuses on the interplay of repetition and difference alive in all creative processes including the use of language and thus in any attempt to know or become educated. Critiquing traditional perspectives on representation that emphasize sameness and identity (in Plato, for example) or the simple relation between a model and its copy, Deleuze insists that the energy internal to repetition is difference. In other words, he sees in this relation a destablizing force, an affirmative energy necessary to all transformation.

Deleuze looks carefully at the elements operating in all attempts to create. For example, I decide to paint grapevine around my kitchen door. As a model, I use some vine from behind my garage and begin to paint. We might say that I am attempting to reproduce or repeat the motif of the grapevine, but is this what happens? I look at a leaf, its shape and color, and back at the wall where I create a shape, looking again at the vine and back at the wall to add to the paint already there in the attempt to make my idea of a grapevine. Am I reproducing the grapevine? Deleuze argues that in this process of painting the artist combines "an element of one instance with another element of a following instance" introducing "a disequilibrium into the dynamic process of construction, an instability, dissymetry or gap of some kind which disappears only in the overall effect" (1994, pp. 19–20).

I look at the result of my effort with a certain satisfaction: ah, a grapevine! The overall effect remains stable, a static repetition of the vine. Yet, there is also a dynamic, positive repetition caused by the differences occurring in the spaces between one look and the next and between one brush stroke and the next. The idea of "vineness" is a dynamic one caused by these differential moments.

Analyzing this process, Deleuze explains that there are two simultaneous repetitive structures occurring. "One refers back to a single concept, which leaves only an external difference between the ordinary instances of a figure; the other is the repetition of an internal difference which it incorporates in each of its moments, and carries from one distinctive point to another" (1994, p. 19). The vine I paint is identifiable as a grapevine, and I'm pleased for that. A concept of sameness allows that experience. My rendition is also obviously different, not the vine itself, and so I also discern a difference between these objects resulting from the repetition. Yet, according to Deleuze, this difference is but an external material shell, a difference between objects, based on the concept of identity and sameness. "It hides a more fundamental operation resulting from the constancy of a dynamic internal movement of difference, which unfolds as pure movement, creative of a dynamic space and time which correspond to the Idea" (p. 20).

My painting of the grapevine unfolds as, moment to moment, stroke by stroke, I combine elements of my perception of the model vine with the paint on the wall. While the concept of grapevine may remain stable, the "Idea" is never stable due to this dynamic differentiating process occurring in my attempt to paint—and in all attempts to create including pedagogy. In his examination of these two views of repetition, Deleuze opens us to the connection between our attempts to interpret the world and a larger generative force:

> The first repetition is repetition of the Same, explained by the identity of the concept or representation; the second includes difference, and includes itself in the alterity of the Idea. . . . One is negative, occurring by default in the concept; the other is affirmative, *occurring by excess* in the Idea. . . . One is developed and explicated, the other enveloped and in need of interpretation. . . . One is material, the other spiritual even in nature and in the earth. One is inanimate, the other carries the secret of our deaths and our lives, of our enchainments and our liberations. . . . (1994, p. 24).

During the eight hours of painting in my kitchen, I felt something inexplicable coursing through me, pushing me on and on as a dancing vine appeared on the wall. When I finished, I said to a friend, "My gosh! I don't know where this came from!" in much the same awe as I experienced when my students passionately took over the class discussion. I didn't mean just the representation of the vine. I meant the entire process that had accomplished it and my experience of it—the simultaneous excitement and serenity.

Without understanding this at that moment, I was responding to the very dynamic described by Deleuze, a creative, dynamic, even spiritual event produced through repetition and difference. And this, I believe, is exactly what happens in classrooms and pedagogical relations of all kinds all the time. We are constantly dealing with and participating in this excessive generative life force, whether conscious of it or not. Teachers put out information and meanings that they hope and even expect their students will consider, understand, and even repeat. What actually gets created in the process of understanding, however, even in the most precise renditions, is always something else at the same moment it is a repetition. And this, as I will show in more detail below, is because of the moving paradoxical force of difference.

According to Deleuze, this paradoxical dynamic is often disconcerting because it defies any linear, rational explanation common to our interpretations of the way things work. That which is repeated is simultaneously same and different, producing a paradox of sense. "Good sense affirms that in all things there is a determinable sense or direction (sens); but paradox is the affirmation of both senses or directions at the same time. . . . Paradox is initially that which destroys good sense as the only direction, but it is also that which destroys common sense as the assignation of fixed identities" (1990, pp. 1–3).

Throughout this book, I explore this paradoxical process of repetition and difference using the post-structuralist analysis of translation, which has interesting implications for thinking about culture and knowledge and, more specifically, about the importance of the teaching-learning relation. While many theorists have written about the importance of dialogue or conversation for exploring the liberatory possibilities in pedagogy, I prefer the notion of translation because, as I discuss below, it includes within it a paradoxical sense of repetition, both creation and movement.

As teachers, we tell students what we believe to be important. We tell them our stories and they tell us theirs, but that's not all. Those stories are always a matter of repetition and difference in the Deleuzian sense. They are translations and thus transformations. It is never a simple exchange or representation; something gets made in the repetitive process. The details of how this works and the varieties of contexts in which its unpredictable effects circulate are what *Seeking Passage* is about. Though my approach may not be a commonsense view of any of these terms, I think of translation in this book as both metaphor and method, as a specific kind of passage making between the text of my life, philosophy, and education.

Pedagogy and/as Translation

The ambiguities in words or the residue of meaning caused by their relationships to each other makes them necessarily irreplaceable and hence essentially un-translatable. This paradoxical un-translatability within translation is too often considered a failure, and so it is, if we are inclined to think of success only in terms of the transferability of some essential or original meaning.

Quite apart from this negative interpretation of truth and meaning, what we find in post-structural thought is an affirmative attitude about this so-called failure, a sense of the beauty and joyful possibility that results from this paradoxical excess. Postmodern philosopher and essayist José Ortega y Gasset calls this "the misery and splendor of translation," referring to any attempt to translate, and indeed any attempt to know, as a necessarily utopian endeavor:

> Isn't the act of translating necessarily a utopian task? The truth is, I've become more and more convinced that everything Man does is utopian. Although he is

principally involved in trying to know, he never fully succeeds in knowing any-thing. When deciding what is fair, he inevitably falls into cunning. He thinks he loves and then discovers he only promised to. Don't misunderstand my words to be a satire on morals, as if I would criticize my colleagues because they don't do what they propose. My intention is, precisely, the opposite; rather than blame them for their failure, I would suggest that none of these things can be done, for they are impossible in their very essence. . . . (quoted in Schulte and Biguenet, 1992, p. 93)

This "misery and splendor" in translation is a nice analogy for the tension I was mentioning earlier. A teacher may have clear goals and objectives, but what happens is never exactly what was planned. Differences are always at play to see to that.

When a translator attempts to translate a text, she strives to repeat in another language what the original text has said. Yet, the translation is never a pure repetition or copy, since through her reading and rewriting, something different is necessarily introduced into the text. "Translation," writes Maurice Blanchot, "is the sheer play of difference: it constantly makes allusion to dif-ference, dissimulates difference, but by occasionally revealing and often ac-centuating it, *translation becomes the very life of this difference*" (quoted in Venuti, 1992, p. 13; emphasis added). This operation of difference is what Derrida calls "the being language of language," making translation (and teach-ing) both possible and impossible (1985b, p. 124).

Translation changes the "original" at least twice, and this is the very ba-sis of the text's survival, its life as a text (Derrida, 1979). We might say that this is the very basis of the life of thought, of knowledge, and of culture. Fur-ther, I will argue that pedagogy is at the heart of this life-giving difference, responsible for the creation of thought and of culture.

Let's say that the teacher is the translator. When a teacher teaches, she tries rigorously to repeat the meaning in a given text, but what she says to her students is never exactly the same; it is necessarily a translation and therefore "other." She takes up a text to be taught and in the very teaching process trans-lates that text (body of knowledge, signs, meanings, discourses); that is, she puts it in her own words, adds her own stories or questions, her own intona-tions and gestures, and transforms it. According to Deleuze's reasoning, there is in her repetitive gesture the operation of an affirmative differentiating force.

The notion of passage making is again useful. In trying to teach, we cre-ate a passage from one text to the other, from the native tongue into the tongue of another. And even while we struggle to (and may assume that we do) re-peat the original rigorously, something new is always created in the passage, "and for the notion of translation we would have to substitute a notion of transformation: a regulated transformation of one language by another, of one text by another" (Derrida, 1985b, p. 95).

Because of this dynamic differential process, the text taught or translated is never exactly replicated by the teacher's words. The ambiguities or multiple meanings of the first text, those excess meanings created in the peculiar relations among the words themselves and their reading, can never be strictly replicated in the translation. Moreover, the second text, the teacher's lecture or interpretation, will have its own ambiguities. It is the existence of difference itself or, as Serres would say, the presence of the third person that survives in any communication or translation. And the students must in turn take up the text and put it in their own words, that is, translate it again, wherein they too will invent new thinking or gestures or questions. To invent is not to produce, it is to translate (Serres, 1982). Knowledge is the result of this generative pedagogic process, passages made from one creative form to another and another in a long historical series. "All learning demands this voyage with the other toward alterity. During this passage, lots of things change" (Serres, 1997, p. 48).

The teacher, as a translator in a long line of translations responding to the demand for survival by the text, assures its growth, its movement, its life. In turn, the students as translators can only augment this dynamic. Rather than assuring the successful reception of the text, the students engage its growth and transformation through the play of differential excess and the noisy third. Thus, as Serres teaches us, the world is composed of "beautiful noise" and such relational nomadic play initiates passages toward different ways of being.

This nomadic dynamic is not due to any ethical law or determination within the teaching-learning process. Rather, the differentially generated movement that ensures inventions of all kinds and thus the "living on" of text, knowledge, and culture happens whether we intend it or are totally unaware of it. It is not a matter of deciding to modify thought, but rather an inevitable effect of trying to communicate something, that is, to teach something to someone else. The process assures that predictability and prescription, and thus control of the outcome of teaching, will always be, strictly speaking, impossible. The differential force is simply always operating.

It is precisely on this basis that education is often erroneously defined as a second-class discipline, and schools as weak and failing institutions. Or, as Deleuze would say, this is why education is both "amorous and fatal." It never succeeds just as one plans, and yet it is often quite beautiful and even powerful nonetheless.

A personal story helps to illuminate this dynamic. For several years, I was a choreographer for young figure skaters, a vocation that I dearly loved. I put together "programs" (figure skating lingo for the moves or dance set to music) and then set out to teach them to the skaters. The children would take the series of gestures that I created for them and work hard to get them "right."

Of course, their interpretations of the moves—no matter how talented they were at skating—were never precisely what I had created for them. With each repetition (or translation) of the series of moves, each attempt to perfect the program, more differences in the gestures were made. For example, an arm and hand might be slightly more curved, a leg a bit higher. No matter what my intentions had been, the skater's performance was always necessarily different from what I might have predicted or even desired.

While a performance might be judged a disaster, I was often deeply touched, even awestruck by the beauty of a particular gesture. This awe and joy, the aesthetic experience, is precisely the result of the unpredictable, differential effects created in the passage between the choreographer's "text," and the skater's translation of it. This process of repetition and difference and the resulting joy (or frustration) is exactly what happens between teachers and students in classrooms, too. The possibility for new ideas, new knowledge, and new beauty is dependent upon it. This is the process that I define in this book as pedagogy, using translation as both metaphor and method.

While I am certain that possibilities for new knowledge and different ways of living inhere in this process, and while I know I have experienced intense joy as a result, I must emphasize that there is nothing inherently good or beautiful about the generative spirit within the pedagogic relation. Deleuze warns us of becoming enraptured by a notion of difference that only expresses the "good" (1994, p. xx). Forces of differentiation are not held by any inherent moral law or sentiment of good will. Both Deleuze and Serres ask us to understand the power of difference to challenge every model and hence to be aware of its sheer aggressive force. For Deleuze, even negation must be included in what is possible in this differentiating process. Rather than its opposite, negation is to be understood as part of the affirmative active force of difference:

> The negative is not present in the essence as that from which force draws its activity: on the contrary it is a result of activity, of the existence of an active force and affirmation of its difference. The negative is a product of existence itself: the aggression necessarily linked to an active existence, the aggression of an affirmation. (1983, p. 9)

Thus Deleuze does not simply offer yet another set of oppositions—between difference and negation, the paradoxical and the dialectical, or affirmation and aggression. Difference is the generative force in every possible struggle and every outcome, those we may determine to be beautiful and amorous as well as those we may find to be destructive or fatal. And this is exactly why we must define education as something other than pedagogy.

While there is nothing inherent within the pedagogical dynamic that points us toward the "good," the process of becoming educated demands attention to questions of how to live ethically, how to choose together from among all the possible outcomes, even while accepting that there are no certain answers. It demands particularly that we face the forms of suffering that are created within the world.

Ethics and Pedagogy

Ethics must be all teachers' willingness to constantly ask what our work means in relation to a whole range of social, political, and cultural forces, and our willingness to shift our behaviors, our beliefs, and our identities as we come to understand the implications of what we do as political, transformative work. It means that we must care for the truth as an infinite translational process and thus must be always in the process of becoming different. I'm inspired to think about the relation between pedagogy and ethics by the straightforward and simple words of Michel Foucault, who asks:

> What can the ethics of an intellectual be . . . if not . . . to render oneself permanently capable of self-detachment . . . ? To be at the same time an academic and an intellectual is to try to engage a type of knowledge and analysis that is taught and received in the university in a way so as to modify not only the thought of others but one's own as well. (1989, p. 303)

Self-detachment is a willingness to question one's entrenched points of view, to subject one's identity to an analytic interpretive process, and to distance oneself from those positions if necessary. Obviously, this requires the courage to read and think about the specificity of our lives, to carefully reflect upon our particular beliefs, commitments, and practices as well as the larger context within which those have been shaped. An ethical orientation requires taking the steps necessary to change our lives, to detach from old habits and practices that make us who we are, and to imagine new ways of being. In this book I use autobiography as such a vehicle of self-detachment, looking at and writing about moments in my life in order to assert questions and re-create myself as an educator and theorist.

I am a teacher educator. Every semester I ask my undergraduate students to join me in a collective and personal struggle with the question, What does it mean to become educated? I ask them this because I believe that people who teach must be able to reflect upon that question, not in order to come to some final or certain answer, but to constantly challenge themselves to be conscious of what they *are* doing in relation to what they believe they *ought to be* doing. This is an interpretive process that involves questions of the good. I believe strongly that this process must be engaged on a closely personal level, that is, introspectively and autobiographically, as well as in relation to larger theoretical frameworks that analyze both broad and specific social, historical, and cultural contexts.

Of all professionals, educators ought to be able to think about who they have been, who they are becoming, and what the world they live in has to do with any of this. Moreover, they ought to be in the habit of asking what their relation to and experience of the larger world around them has to do with what they believe about teaching and learning, about education, and therefore what they believe education offers a person or a community or the larger world. They ought to be able to ponder what kind of person the world needs and thus make choices for what they ought to be doing in their own classrooms. If they don't, someone else surely will.

So when I say that, for me, a definition of education as a workable concept includes ethics, I mean to make an important distinction between the concepts of pedagogy and education. I include in my sense of what it means to become educated a willingness to confront suffering and to engage difficult questions around "the collective good" in one's personal life, in classrooms, in communities, in the world, while recognizing that there are no certain or final answers.

Each semester, as I engage this difficult question with my undergraduates, at least one wise student protests that she cannot determine what it means to become educated because this would mean that she would have to "judge" someone else's life. Ah, the heart of the matter! When I first met with this response, I jumped in and said, "Yes! Of course you must judge. How can you educate and not judge?" I still believe this to be true. At the same time, I share my students' concerns about the dangers of taking an authoritarian stand in relation to knowledge, the dangers of saying "I know what it means, and thus you must listen to me." Yet, there are real dangers in taking the opposite, "anything goes" position as well. Many of my students are so steeped in the relativist position of "my opinion is as valid as your opinion" that they cannot see any other response.

There are probably developmental reasons for this, as argued by those interested in democratic, antiracist, feminist, and other social justice orientations to education (Alschuler, 1980; Spring, 2000). When confronted with daunting social problems or questions such as the one I pose, students go through certain predictable phases beginning with denial or defensiveness (often blaming others) and moving through a sense of overwhelming uncertainty or powerlessness before being able to see a means of action or resolution. The steps go something like this: (1) This is not my problem; I don't have to look at it. (2) This may be an important question, but I am powerless to do anything about it. Besides, I have my opinion and you have yours. (3) OK. I see the problem and am willing to look for ways I can work to resolve it.

My students often seem to be stuck in the middle phase, where they may agree that there are reasons to act, but fear their ability to be effective, or even their right to take a stand. They are, of course, not alone in their fear. Our culture is experiencing an important shift in perspective and understanding resulting from a major challenge to the frameworks that have shaped our sense making for centuries. Jean François Lyotard (1988) has dubbed this dilemma the postmodern condition, namely, to be so skeptical of the "master narratives" or truths that have previously framed the meaning of Western civilization that there is no longer any certain basis or foundation for judgment. Unfortunately for my students, this uncertainty is too often paralyzing.

"Hmm, I think I see the difficulty," I say. "How can you possibly know the truth of this matter and determine it for someone else without being authoritarian and imposing some version of the truth on someone else? And yet, how can we teach if we don't know what we are aiming for, if anybody's opinion on something is as good as anyone else's?" I go to the board and draw a continuum. On one end is what I call (to their discomfort) the terrorist position: Someone claims to have the "truth" (about who the true God is, about the meaning of life, or about what it means to become educated, for example) and demands allegiance to that truth under threat of punishment. On the other extreme is the nihilist position: There is no truth, so therefore anyone's truth is as valid as anyone else's, and anything goes; essentially, nothing matters. In hearty rejection of the terrorist position, the student who first raised the question had jumped into the nihilist boat, but now she wasn't sure: "It's not true that nothing matters, but who has the truth? How do we decide?" Indeed.

While I do not pretend that there exist any fast answers to the big questions like "what is the good?" I do want to insist that part of what it means to become educated (and this surely includes becoming a teacher) requires that we struggle with that question while accepting that there are no final answers. What is a good life for me and for this larger community? What must I do, how must I change to move in that direction? What must I teach myself and others? Approaching these questions is like stepping up to the edge of an abyss where there is nothing to discover. All bridges must be created for safe passage across this differential space.

Teaching, Thinking, and the Problem of Value

To teach is always to be in the process of creating something with someone. Usually it is about creating thinking even if we don't know (can't know) precisely what that thinking will be. To teach well is to push for thinking, to inspire it, to generate it, which is not to say that when we teach we know exactly what the other will think or create. Rather, to teach is to set in motion forces that are creative of all kinds of thought about all kinds of questions.

To teach as a practice of becoming educated is also to take the responsibility for engaging a selective process, a process of valuing, and evaluating values. We engage others' values in relation to our own, we engage our own values, and we take responsibility for critiquing those so as to create different values. For Buddhists, to engage the question of values is to confront the problem of suffering, for whether and how we value others directly affects the quality of their lives. As I will develop in this book, teaching for social justice requires that we and our students look at how our values affect others. To teach this way is the act of becoming educated as we educate. And this is where ethics and pedagogy intersect.

No matter what our intentions, whether we are teaching as a conscious act of social transformation or not, we cannot be actively engaged in teaching without actively engaging values, our own and those of others. We may even deny that we do so in the name of good, objective, value-free, or neutral teaching. I am arguing that to become educated is to engage the problem of values consciously, to be attentive and selective, to choose among values as a matter of compassion and awakening. To become educated is to choose how to live, how to become, which is to say, how to be as a matter of movement and creation of self or, as Foucault says, as a matter of self-detachment.

To teach well, that is, to be an ethically and socially committed educator, is to insist on and to assist others in becoming responsible for this self-detaching engagement, to attend to and to pose the questions necessary to creating new ways of thinking and better ways of living in the world. As before, I use the term *self-detachment* to point to processes by which we may become different and thus engage different practices. It is always a process of engaging values, of evaluating values, not as imposition, but rather as creative movement toward better ways of being.

Thus we attend to the problem of suffering, survival, and well-being in both a personal and collective sense. We attend by examining our own lives—the values, meanings, and beliefs that guide us—and by detaching from values that we may deem harmful. This is always a process of critique and the possibility for seeing differently, and thus is creative. That is, it is not simply a matter of "becoming conscious" but rather a matter of becoming different. Ethics always depend upon the generative pedagogical force.

Gilles Deleuze again helps us to see that creation is always a matter of differentiation and thus of evaluation. In order to see differently, we must evaluate:

> The notion of value implies a critical reversal. On the one hand values appear or are given as principles: and evaluation presupposes values on the basis of

which phenomena are appraised. But, on the other hand and more profoundly, it is values which presuppose evaluations, "perspectives of appraisal," from which their own value is derived. The problem of critique is that of the value of values, of the evaluation from which their value arises, thus the problem of their creation. *Evaluation is defined as the differential element of corresponding values, an element which is both critical and creative.* Evaluations in essence are not values but ways of being, modes of existence of those who judge and evaluate, serving as principles for the values on the basis of which they judge. This is why we always have the beliefs, feelings and thoughts that we deserve given our way of being and our style of life. (1983, p. 1, emphasis added)

Here Deleuze makes clear the critical relation between processes of differentiation, values, and an ethical mode of existence. That is, to engage the world and oneself ethically, to put oneself in the position of evaluating what is good for self and others, is to differentiate this from that and thus to create. It is to seek, to set in motion the creative affirmative process of differentiation through thinking about what else could be possible for the world.

In her analysis of the trial of Adloph Eichmann, henchman of the Third Reich condemned to death for ordering the murder of hundreds of thousands of Jews during World War II, Hannah Arendt argues that this form of evaluation is what must be understood as thinking, and is the only protection against the banality of evil (Gordon, 1988). Eichmann, she argues, was incapable of such a form of thinking. His thought processes were limited to a technical-rational, means-ends process that did not require consideration of the good.

Uncertain as it is, the good is nothing more or less than the result of our singular and collective translational efforts around its infinite definition. This unending process is precisely where education and freedom intersect. Teaching is a form of professional praxis, a constant process of question making and answer seeking, of reading and writing and conversing as translation. And when those questions include matters of social, personal, and ecological welfare, pedagogy engages a practical ethics and becomes the practice of freedom. In the words of John Dewey, "We are free not because of what we statically are, but insofar as we are becoming something different from what we have been" (1960, p. 280).

Freedom is not a result of "anything goes," but rather of constant evaluation and reevaluation of our practices, beliefs, and habits—a constant reading and rewriting of our lives in relation to others—and of engaging differences as a matter of seeking better ways of living together on this earth. As praxis, to teach and to learn form an event we call *pedagogy*, the effects of which become part of the "beautiful noise," as Serres would say. And yet, for there to be *education*, there must be more than noise. We must look for the passages that would lead us to better ways of living.

To become educated requires that we are engaged with others in confronting the problem of suffering and well-being, examining what is good for ourselves and our communities and for our earth and her creatures. And this is tricky business for the very reasons that Derrida, Serres, Deleuze, and others warn us of. There is no original, fundamental, or universal truth about the best government or schools or classroom methods or behaviors to be found, but rather infinite differences in perception and interpretation of the problems, as well as in articulations of the solutions.

Once again we find ourselves confronted with a tension between the knowledge that we may never find the perfect solution and the ongoing necessity to create the best possible conditions for life in our communities. We and our students must learn to struggle over our own perceptions, interpretations, behaviors, beliefs, and so forth, as well as those of our colleagues, teachers, and neighbors. This is one place where autobiography as a method of educational research and practice can be very useful.

Ethics, Autobiography, and Pedagogy

Proceed then, by seeking out the edges, the inner walls, the passages.

—Jacques Derrida

I treat autobiographical writing as a particular form of translation, a paradoxical process of repetition and difference that could open a certain sensitivity to one's own joys and suffering and thus connect one to the larger world. Such sensitivity is necessary to the opening of an ethical relation with the world, a relation of caring for the other. As translation, a form where we try to repeat rigorously an "original" text—in this case our lives—autobiography can be understood to be a transformative performance (Derrida, 1985b; Nussbaum, 1990); it is never a matter of relating the truth of one's life but is always a matter of fashioning a story, a fiction functioning as truth. One writes one's life as a kind of problematic repetition of what has gone before, using a language or a "voice" necessarily different from that used before. As in other translations, the result is never, strictly speaking, a pure repetition; there are always differences at play. As Derrida would say, *differánce* is always operating to deconstruct the text. For this reason, autobiography as the representation of one's life is, strictly speaking, impossible.

Although autobiography is generally thought of as a self-representational process, the self, as both the subject and object of this writing, is never present nor simply re-presented. Rather, the "I" that is the subject of these stories is part of the creative, differential process of the reading and writing dynamic. One writes the story of one's self, but what really gets written is something quite different, or other. Thus, autobiography is a process of self-detachment. Or, put another way, it could be that through the autobiographical translation of our lives, we attempt to "live on" (A. Benjamin, 1992; Derrida, 1979).

So while I struggle throughout this book to keep my own voice strong and present as I listen carefully to the theorists who are my teachers, it is really not so much a matter of holding onto or even discovering my voice as it is one of creating it, that is, of creating myself as I wind through the labyrinth of memory, pushing questions to the edge and seeking passage to somewhere else.

As autobiographical essayist Nancy Mairs (1994) writes, "the voice in question, like the woman called into being to explain its existence, is an invention" (p. 16). Using autobiography as a form of research, we explore questions and write our lives. And as we do, we invent ourselves over and over again. The reinvention of self is possible precisely because of the operation of differences alive in the attempt to think, in the spaces between the actual event, our memory of it, and the stories we tell.

These spaces and the differences created therein provide us with openings to new ways of thinking, to the possibility of living ethically, of caring for each other. They open us to the challenge of becoming different and hence to the possibility of changing the world. As I said earlier, the creation of such openings to a better world, to a more ethical way of life through rigorous attention to questions or problems, including those in our own lives, is where education circulates.

As Maxine Greene (1978) has taught us, teachers with their students have to begin to love the questions. Those who would claim the existence of foundational truth or knowledge transmitted in specific canonized texts, or even those invested in critical theoretical positions who put their faith for emancipation in metatheories of dialectical thought will be disappointed or frustrated when confronted with such paradoxical results as I have been trying to describe in this chapter. Education promises to succeed, but its success is always a supplement; it therefore breaks its promise and fails, or at least that's what we think. And as long as we view such supplementarity and excess noise as a failure, education will always be viewed as, and play its part as, a second-rate discipline.

Fundamentally interested in making the world a more just, more equitable, and more environmentally healthy place to live, the essays that comprise *Seeking Passage* seek to describe the specific generative dynamic that is the result of the teaching-learning relation, a translational relation creative of the possibilities we must learn to choose from. I believe that if classroom teachers, school administrators, and teacher educators were to understand

and attend carefully to this process, the actual transformational possibilities that inhere there would be more effective.

How do we begin to grapple with the multitude of possibilities that get made in the process of teaching-learning relations; and, how do we ask our students to grapple with issues of justice, environmental responsibility, suffering, and social welfare in the face of such overwhelming uncertainty and possibility? Clearly, as Serres teaches us, the journey is not easy. The passages are narrow and dangerous.

To make a journey, one must leave home, depart, cut oneself off from what is familiar and safe. So while there is joy and exhilaration, there is also fear caused by the perils of self-imposed exile. Exhilaration and exile. The prefix *ex-* means to be outside. I know the discomfort of outsiderness. And yet I agree strongly with Serres:

> No learning can avoid the voyage. Under the supervision of a guide, education pushes one to the outside. Depart: go forth. Leave the womb of your mother, the crib, the shadow cast by your father's house and the landscapes of your childhood. In the wind, in the rain: the outside has no shelters. . . . Learning launches wandering. (1997, p. 8)

To put oneself on the path of education is to become a nomad in the search for passages toward more just ways of being. Autobiography demands a kind of doubling back, to gaze at one's childhood homeland from the vantage of a distant hillside, as a means of moving on, preferably toward spaces and ways of living that are better for oneself and for the larger world. As I will try to show in this book, nomadic movement, along with the necessity to choose well how one will dwell with others, is what pedagogy creates and what the transformation of the world demands.

Chapter 2

Leaving Home

December 29, 1992
My dear River friend,

I have been living a kind of split existence for many years. With you I experience a connection that has claimed a very important piece of my soul. You are the River, and I am more tied in love and reverence to you than words can describe. This is a love of the earth and her water, of a beautiful place and the time spent there. In your arms I have felt cradled by this reverence, profoundly at home.

And yet not at home. And this because of another pull in my life that has nothing to do with that place, that is something much less tangible, incorporeal, and yet so real for me that it cannot be denied. This other love has haunted me since childhood. It is about questions, about wonder, about thought, about ideas, about words, about the world, the universe, myself. And it takes me away from home, the River, toward a home that has no place. A place that is profoundly no place. Joyous beyond anything I have ever experienced and yet very, very lonely.

And so dear friend, it is with great difficulty that I write. It's time for me to leave home.

As long as I can remember, I have enjoyed a very strong emotional and spiritual attachment to the St. Lawrence River, in particular to a forty-mile span of the River known as the Thousand Islands. As a child, I spent many weekends playing at the River's edge, listening to the lullabies created by the water's caressing of the shore, sharing ideas with her, dreaming of what my life might be. I later fell in love among the Island's passages, still enthralled by the River's songs, and still asking her my questions. I married, and after several years of commuting three hours back to the River nearly every weekend, my husband and I moved to a small community whose soul is indelibly inscribed upon the banks of this beautiful and powerful body of water.

Now, as a scholar interested in the dynamic generative process of education, I find myself thinking back upon that moving aquatic body, my historical attachment there, and the painful process of leaving her shores as I grew into the future that I had dreamed of as a child. In my work I engage questions derived from my own life as a means of getting at the heart of what we might understand education to be. This particular writing is an attempt to find a passage between three terms—translation, curriculum, and autobiography—by thinking through the experience of leaving home. I am looking for a way to make sense of this specific experience in my life, an experience of leaving a place that I love, in order to say something else, something about my commitment to the moving, generative process of education.

The writing is a translation of a piece of my life, and since texts under translation never remain "at home" in the "mother tongue," it will necessarily be a leaving too. In this sense, autobiography, like translation, is a process of transformation necessitated by the very attempt to rewrite a text, in this case, the text of my life. As translation, a form where we try to repeat rigorously an original text, autobiography can be understood to be a transformative performance (Derrida, 1985b). One writes one's life as a kind of re-presentation of what has gone before, and yet, as in other translations, the result is never, strictly speaking, a pure repetition; there are always differences which move us both emotionally and from place to place.

Autobiography as translation is just this sort of leaving, a moving from one text to another, as well as from one psychological experience or self-understanding to another. Such a moving process can open sensitivity to one's own joys and suffering, as well as to the experiences of others, and thus to the possibility of new ways of living. The creation of such openings to a better world and to a more ethical way of life through rigorous attention to questions or problems, including those in our own lives, is where education circulates. Consequently, I see the use of autobiography as a method for thinking about education.

In the analysis below, I explore the difficult process of detaching from one's homeland, in particular from geographical attachments, as a means of transforming one's life. This writing, a translation of a moment in my own life, serves as both a metaphor for and an example of what I believe is at the heart of the educational process. I wonder about leavings and arrivals, detachments and attachments of all kinds that mark the paths of our lives, and the moving that creates them. I think about this moving as it happens within educational relations. And though I can't be sure of the destination exactly, I know this particular translational journey is about my own education.

Home

> "So-this-is-a River!"
> "The River," corrected the Rat.
> "And you really live by the river? What a jolly life!"
> "By it and with it and on it and in it," said the Rat. "It's brother
> and sister to me, and aunts and company, and food and drink,
> and (naturally) washing. It's my world, and I don't want any other.
> What it hasn't got is not worth having, and what it doesn't know
> is not worth knowing. Lord! the times we've had together!"
> —Kenneth Grahame

I have always loved this passage in the *Wind in the Willows* (1987). I understand the Rat, his keen sense of the sweet enclosure made around his life by the River. "By it and with it and on it and in it," the Rat is embraced by and embraces the River, and he makes clear to the Mole the specificity of his attachment. Not any river, this place, *The* River. His declaration honors the smells, the sounds, the entire sensual experience of his relation to this place, making it more than a river. In his declaration the Rat gives significance to the relation between himself, the Earth, the water, and all that occurs there. His words given to and heard by the Mole attach him to the force of movement made by water and Earth, honoring the life-sustaining forces there and defining his own life through them. "Lord! The times we've had together!" Thus, he honors this place, creating it as home.

Our sense of home is an attachment that does not get made outside our attempts to read and to write, to say something about our relation to a particular location, to read a particular landscape and to express our care for it, and perhaps for each other in it. As I remember for myself and you the squeak and bang of the old screen door at my grandmother's camp on the St. Lawrence River, and the way the water lapping the shore put me to sleep in the hot sunny room upstairs, or the summer I fell in love in the romantic passages made by the Islands, I create and re-create the texture of this homeplace. I ask you to listen as I weave loving autobiographical boundaries around the geography as I read and reread it.

We search for what is legible in the bodies of water and the shorelines and hills, the desert sands, or the city streets in a search for connection to particular geographical locations and the lives that exist there. As Deborah Tall writes, "I read the landscape to help me through, to know what's come before me there, to find my footing in time. The land can speak us back to ourselves, a kind of autobiography" (1995, p. 25). For Tall this is a conscious project, a systematic effort to create an attachment and make a home for herself in a new geographical location. We all read the landscape, or in my case the waterscape, though probably seldom so consciously, as we seek geographical comfort and create attachments to certain places. But it is more than reading. It is always writing, too; we write our relationship to the Earth and to each other. We write ourselves into it, as Tall suggests, through "a kind of autobiography."

We read, and in turn, we tell our stories, we make our maps and our gardens, we design our living spaces, we create rituals that produce us within meaningful relations, attachments to each other and to specific localities that we call home.

bell hooks tells of black women's historical work at making homeplaces, describing the construction of affirmation and safety within their houses.

> In our young minds houses belonged to women, were their special domain, not as property, but as places where all that truly mattered in life took place—the warmth and comfort of shelter, the feeding of our bodies, the nurturing of our souls. There we learned dignity, integrity of being; there we learned to have faith. . . .
>
> The task of making a homeplace was . . . about the construction of a safe place where black people could affirm one another. . . .
>
> I want to remember these black women today. The act of remembrance is a conscious gesture of honoring their struggle. . . . (1990, pp. 42–43)

Here hooks describes women's discursive practice, made of specific gestures that "made life happen," gestures that, as they were read by others and here by hooks herself, functioned to define this enclosure as a "homeplace."

Home is thus textual; it has a "*texture*" made of gestures, words, symbolic objects, and practices of all kinds. It is woven through with a kind of testamentary structure by which we declare our attachment to a particular location, to a neighborhood, a piece of the Earth, or the banks of a river, through our everyday conversations and practices with others. We tell each other of our lives, we declare our sense of home to ourselves and others, and a kind of moving weave develops. This weave depends on and is constituted by the reading or hearing of the other. As Derrida has taught us, there is no text outside its reading. I'm reminded of a graduate school colleague's inquiries after I had moved to Michigan for my first job. "Is there a river?" Tony Whitson asked. I was surprised by his insight and deeply touched by his kindness. "Yes," I said, "but not *The* River."

As we create a sense of attachment to a place through our textured relation to it, we begin to honor it and the people who inhabit it. We do so by telling our stories which are further read and retold. Thus it is that both place as home and our own autobiographies are produced. I'm translating my life.

I'm making a passage between geography and biography. It is in and through the gesture of honoring the location that it "takes place" and becomes significant. Here I honor the River in your presence as having been my home, and as you receive and make sense of this gesture, both the moving text of my life, the River, and her people are affirmed. In this way home and the real psychological experience of it becomes multilayered and complex, constantly reshaped and thus in flux by virtue of our discursive lives.

So, in an odd, paradoxical way, although we think of home as that enclosure which most ensures safety and warmth, there is nothing inherently stable or certain about it or our relation to it. Indeed, precisely due to its textuality, its constant state of being read and reread, home forms part of a structure that is inherently nomadic.

Place as Pause

Cultural geographer Yi-Fu Tuan uses the concepts of spaces and pauses to elucidate this nomadic quality of home: "If we think of space as that which allows movement, then place is pause; each pause in movement makes it possible for location to be transformed into place" (1977, p. 6). As Derrida and other post-structural philosophers have taught us, any text or textual relation is characterized by a kind of indefinite supplementary movement or mobility, made possible by the space between the signifier and the signified, or between the writing and the reading. This relational space is what creates the text, and this includes our sense of home.

Before there is a place, before there is home, there is a space, the indeterminate, the unknown of no-place. It is when we create boundaries and mark off territory with our words and other representational forms that we create places that can then be revered as homes. As a pause, home is marked off by boundaries, depends upon boundaries, which are made by arrivals and leavings, attachments and detachments. Thus, home is an event; it "takes place" through a pause in the nomadic process, the arrivings and leavings that make up our lives. Any arrival and therefore any place is dependent upon such a pause; but pause implies another move, a repetition of movement, and therefore a leaving. Thus it is that the boundaries by which we mark off territory to be called home are made uncertain by the very possibility of leaving.

The difference between to arrive and to pause is movement, that is, nomadic difference. To pause is a kind of arrival but only with the understanding that it is a temporary respite: "Let me rest in your embrace."

Home as place is marked then by an uneasy arrival, and it is the earlier described texture of it, its inscription as a discursive event, that creates it as such. We might say that the discursive process of creating a place as home is the process of boundary marking, and the boundary marking distinguishes this home from that, this group from that.

Think of teachers and students and classrooms. I remember that uneasy feeling of arriving at my new classroom each year as an elementary student. The teacher had worked hard to make it welcoming, but it was not yet a homeplace for me or the others. We had not yet claimed it, marked it as ours, put our stuff on the walls, or heard our names repeated within the space. But within days or perhaps just hours, that room and those people would become a familiar and usually (though not always) safe place, and we claimed it and our teacher as distinctly ours.

We make affiliations connected to these places. I can still remember my third-grade classroom and how happy I felt to be there. Mrs. Munson was special and so were we. I was glad I wasn't in the classroom across the hall. I can even remember teasing students from across the hall that *they* didn't have Mrs. Munson. We differentiate and identify ourselves through such affiliations.

Earlier this century, philospher and social activist Simone Weil (1951) warned about the dangers of such attachments when writing to her friend, a Catholic priest. She refused to be baptized and thus to become part of the Catholic church, even though the ideas of Christianity infused her work and life. Heeding her warning, I want to be careful not to romanticize. There are dangers in this creation of "home." I'm thinking about certain nationalistic as well as academic discourses where the creation of an "us" is organized to exclude and even to kill, where the boundaries are defended to the death. We can imagine "homes" that, though once important enclosures, may cease to be healthy spaces.

Whether or not we heed such dangers, and whether or not they exist, the space beyond the boundaries is always operating to put those lines in question. Every attempt to say or ask something about the territory marked off and the lives or relations within that territory remakes the space inside, shifts the boundaries, and thus redefines, even if slightly, the significance of the place. Again, this is because our saying or our writing is never the simple transmission and reception of information; there is always difference at play. Using terms offered by Deleuze and Guattari (1987), every conceptual territory is constantly in the process of deterritorialization and reterritorialization simply by virtue of our discursive, sense-making, and therefore nomadic relation to it.

Consequently, home as a global, fixed concept or experience is, strictly speaking, impossible; we are indefinitely at home and not. We are always in the process of arriving and leaving, and where we go—the next pause—may be nearer or farther from the last, more beautiful or ugly, better for our lives or worse, depending on any number of unpredictable factors and forces. I mean "unpredictable" in the sense that though we make choices and decisions about the form, direction, speed, and contours of the gestures we make and the texts we weave, we cannot know or predict fully the effects of those discursive practices upon others, upon ourselves, or upon our "homes."

Teachers know this very well. Lovers, too. We write home to the other, and the experiential, textual, territorial shifts that create us depend on and are a result of that distanced reading.

I translate my life. I write to honor a homeplace, to consider its importance. I experience its fragility in my life. I grieve its loss. I am confronted with the very problematic that all translators and all teachers must confront, this movement of language over the border into the language of the other (Derrida, 1979) and "the illusion that all would have been well if we could have just stayed home" (Johnson, 1985, p. 144).

Detachment

We all leave. We are always leaving. Our gardens and our students become the traces of our (and their) comings and goings. I want to know more about this movement, this wandering that is perhaps a more evident part of our lives as teachers and students and scholars than for others, though I'm convinced that nomadism of one sort or another is part of what it means to be human. It is certainly what it takes to become educated—to become different from who we have been and thus to shift the way we live in the world. All becoming different, no matter which direction our journey may take or what forms we may create on the way, is a matter of leaving.

Whatever the circumstances of our leaving, it seems we bring our pain, our homesickness, with us when we embark again, and we strive to cure ourselves by the traces of what we have left. So why did we leave if it is so difficult to let go? If we insist on hanging on to a memory of what was? I believe it is because we are what we have left. Even as we become something else, traces of what we have been stay with us, giving shape and character to our lives and directing the journeys we choose. And if we choose well, we may find purpose to our movement.

This moving, though necessarily disruptive and often painful, is what makes change possible. Detachment is at the heart of education and thus of our ability to think of a better world. We leave home as we search for different relations and ways of being on the earth.

I have mentioned that there is something that is often painful in this process. Even when we leave for the happiest reasons—summer vacation, a new job, a desire to explore, a new love—we still must say good-bye, and it often hurts. The pain is part of the experience of detachment. But let me add that this process of arriving and leaving is also at the heart of the very possibility of joy, and this is because of what happens through the journey of thinking implied by the metaphor of leaving home. Moreover, it is precisely through my attention to this actual experience, my attempt to translate leaving home as a concept that could help me understand education, that I attempt to move out of the pain of leaving the River, and so initiate another kind of leaving.

For me, leaving the River's edge meant leaving year after year of tulips, iris, and bee balm, the accumulation of years of tending to a home, their heralding of that attention spring after spring. I imagine a sad neglect there now and I'm overcome with sadness, an ache, a painful wish that this leaving wasn't so. No longer mine, those gardens will bear the traces of my life and so will speak of me, of my life during those years, until the Earth finally takes back the space. The bulbs and rhizomes mark my history, inscribe the reality of my living; they are its trace.

A stranger coming upon them might ask what stories attach to those garden borders, now growing beyond the carefully edged lines that I drew there in the earth near the River's edge. She might imagine a life there, and passion: passion for the color and texture, the fragrance; passion for the land, the Earth; passion drawn in the dirt, planted there. Once marking my home, that garden is now the sign of my leaving, a tracing of passion caught now in encroaching weeds.

I diverge with this nostalgic passage. Perhaps, I am just trying to detach, to cross the border, to translate my life. But what does it mean? We segment our lives through the creation of specific geographical, social, and personal attachments that never completely leave us. Rather, the traces of these attachments (and detachments) compose us as we engage them. We create loves for the land, for communities, for ideas, for particular souls. We do it on many levels or planes at once, at different speeds, and with different intensities, and those attachments are always subject to disruptions of various strengths, always subject to interrogation. Indeed, as I have already argued, the boundaries of our attachments are in constant flux, whether or not we choose to acknowledge that flux and whether or not we are aware of all the effects of such flux all the time. Detachment is inevitably painful, as Simone Weil teaches us; "there is no detachment where there is no pain. And there is no pain endured, without hatred or lying, unless detachment is present also" (1972, p. 12).

Detachment is a matter of shifting away from certain homeplaces, which may take many forms, such as houses, landscapes, or ideas. Psychological, political, or geographical, these places provide a sense of comfort, so separation may require a kind of grieving. This grieving is a result of the loss of comfort, security, and pleasure that get made relationally in homeplaces—those people, beliefs, rituals, and events that touch us, that move us and teach us. As we leave, a certain sweetness may linger in our hearts.

What is it that comes to push or invite us out of the nest? What allows us to question these homeplaces and our relation to them? Again, Weil's words inspire: "Man only escapes from the laws of this world in lightning flashes. Instants when everything stands still, instants of contemplation, of pure intuition, of mental void, of acceptance of the moral void" (1972, p. 11).

What flashes or intensities of insight invite us to venture forth into the world and hence to risk our sense of security? It could be the excitement of a new adventure, the desire to see the world, or the need to translate—flashes of insight that invite us to translate the meaning of our lives and hence to move on. As Walter Benjamin (1992) says, some texts demand translation in order to "live on." He teaches us that translation is a process through which the life of a text, its richness and its fullness of meaning, is protected. But more, the text is reinvested with meaning and thus with life. Similarly, some lives demand translation in order to live on. Who knows what flash may come as the messenger of such a demand. It is not really predictable. What matters is the nomadic movement of questions and what we do with those questions. Perhaps transformation happens because of our commitments to understand our joy, sorrow, or pain, and so educate ourselves. Leaving home is necessary for such change and growth.

Roots and Rhizomes

Yet, I feel a real tension between the need to grow and to move and a paradoxical need for attachments, for a home—geographical, intellectual, personal. Like the Mole, the wide world beckons relentlessly and undeniably, and yet there is the need to be safe and warm in the familiar.

> He did not want at all to abandon the new life and its splendid spaces, to turn his back on sun and air and all that offered to him and creep home and stay there; the upper world was all too strong, it called him still. . . . But it was good to think he had this to come back to, this place which was all his own. (Grahame, 1987, p. 80)

From my notes written one August while on vacation in the Upper Peninsula in Michigan, I read:

> I'm homesick. I'm looking for a home. I'm yearning for roots even as the rhizome spreads. I like Deleuze's metaphor, but maybe he misses the tension. A rhizome grows along the surface, horizontally, but it also puts down roots as it grows.
>
>   I need to root in the land, and I want to soak in the beauty. I miss the River. But the tension, the desire for growth keeps me moving. Nomadic. Is an inte-

grated life possible? How does one deal with the tension between home and nomadism? Perseid meteors tonight. The stars here make my heart ache. I told them [my friends] that the sky awes me, and they laughed. "This," I said as we looked up, "must be the origin of philosophy." Who are we in relation to this wonder? I want to make an attachment to the beauty of this place, or someplace. I want it to claim me.

Quoting Richard Wilbur, Deborah Tall writes, "Some have the luck to be born and to remain in country which is continuous with their personalities; others ramble about until they can say at last . . . 'this is the place.'" She continues, "If we find it do we know to stay? Is it right for a lifetime?" (Tall, 1993, p. 48). And I wonder: even if we know that a place has claimed our heart and yet we must leave, how do we mend the broken heart of such a separation? What is such an attachment about and what are the consequences of setting out for somewhere else?

It is from the points of disruption in our lives made of flashes from unpredictable sources that we may be able to see differently. It is probably that detachment, necessarily painful, that we need in order to grow, to think, and to live ethically. That is, we need such painful detachment in order to engage the questions: How should I be in the world? How do I care for the other?

We may shrink from this responsibility that leaving home affords us precisely because the pain of detachment is so difficult. We may move toward hatred or indifference. The problem is, how do we use the detachment responsibly, carefully? How do we care for ourselves as we set out, but also, how do we find ways of caring for the world?

Education as Leaving Home

I've learned nothing without leaving, nor taught another without inviting him or her to leave the nest.

—Michel Serres

Pedagogy enacts translation as leaving home. Our pedagogical relations, in whatever contexts we may find them, create the energy needed to embark on the journey. Our interpretations, our questions, and our meaning making push us out across the given boundaries. Leaving home is a way to recommence, to embark again, on the inevitable search for passages toward more ethical and just ways of being in the world. With embarking, we enact a new series of events, a series of places and attachments, traces displaced, carried along, gathered up, a bouquet of homes.

"Maybe," writes Tall, "we need different places for different phases in our lifetime." I'm reminded of William Pinar and Madeline Grumet's (1979) concept of curriculum as *currere*, the life course. I imagine our relation to curriculum as a moving through the homeplaces of our lives in order to translate them, in order that we may live on. To detach and thus to become is to enact, as Deleuze would say, a "line of flight," learning to live on in relation to others and to the Earth and its creatures in ways that allow life to flourish. To live on. To translate. To teach is to engage the possibility of such a translating process.

But how will we recognize the good translation of any given text, including the texts of our own lives? How do we deal with the strict impossibility, yet necessity, of saying something true about a given life? Simone Weil (1956) shows us in her journals that it is in the process of thinking and the attention to truth within the particular sphere of lived experience that we discover the very possibility of life and thus of joy. I write toward such a possibility.

As humans, we tell our stories in order to give ourselves to others and in order to learn something. We tell our friends, our parents, our lovers, our children, and our students what we have done, how we have lived. We ask that they listen. We teach them about ourselves. And we do this at times well and at other times poorly. In short, we create ourselves for others and for ourselves, and it is important that we take care in this process.

Home is who we have made ourselves, and even as we detach, we drag along the traces of attachments to those places: the names, the events that become the stories we tell, the sense of enclosure that they once held for us. Perhaps it is that sense of enclosure that we continue to yearn for, that keeps the search for home alive, that nomadic search. Perhaps it is the buried memory of an original comfort that becomes desire, the trace of enclosure, our mother's womb, an enclosure that once left behind becomes desire for home and continues to fuel this ongoing supplemental process.

This I would call the curriculum of our lives, a long process of nomadic searching, of leaving and translation, and we can do it ethically or not. That is, we can do it with a willingness to self-detach, to modify our thought, and thus to care better for the world and our relation to it. Or we can be less careful. And the difference is not always so easy to discern. How do we care for the other even as we leave? How do we face the anxiety and sorrow of leaving? How do we leave behind attitudes that are not healthy for the world, for the other, as we move toward better ways of living? These are questions that we must ask ourselves and our students.

Students experience great hostility and fear when we ask them to leave the security and comfort of their ideological homes. And yet the end of injustice in the world necessitates that they and we move. The point is, we all must be willing to take the lightning flashes seriously, to engage the translation and thus to re-create, to transform our lives; we must be willing to think even as we risk leaving the security of home. In any case, we are always in the process of leaving.

Perhaps for the flash of lightning we could substitute the lullaby of waves on a shore, or the whispering wind, and if we are as fortunate as the emancipated Mole, each day will be as sunny as his days with Ratty were: "longer and fuller of interest as the ripening of summer moved onward. He learnt to swim and to row, and entered the joy of running water; and with his ear to the reed-stems he caught at intervals, something of what the wind went whispering so constantly among them" (Grahame, 1987, p. 20).

Chapter 3

Choreography and Curriculum Theory

Search for a Passage

What flashes come to move us out of the nest, out of safety?
What could it mean to be moved so powerfully that we are
forced to transform ourselves, our lives, our communities, give
up what has become comfortable, to venture out to create something else? This essay explores that question. And, as I look back
upon the moment that I first wrote it, I see this writing as a
unique "flash" itself. A moment of intense risk, rupture, and
movement in my intellectual life that ultimately led to this book.
It was my first attempt to create something else, to write what
moved me about education. I offer it here as an important re-
flective moment in my life, a flash of blades and ideas across a
hard surface that pushed me both intellectually and personally;
but more important, I offer it as an initial analysis of what goes
on in the transformative moments that move us.

I used to play it safe. Safe within the game space of critical social theory, I
spent my years as a graduate student writing about the politics of knowledge
and exclusion and also about the historical struggles of various marginalized
groups, particularly women, around such exclusion. Strange safety! I wrote
from anger, maybe even vengeance.

I began to think about this in the context of another form of "writing" that
I became very involved in during the latter part of my doctoral program: I choreographed for young figure skaters. Working with youngsters of all shapes and
sizes and ability levels, I found in this work a form that produced great joy.

I was doing choreography during the years when I was writing my dissertation. My dissertation was concerned with the problem of women's dis-

cursive capture in the dualism of mind and body, the way their own writing about education and womanhood recreated age-old forms of domination. I looked at early-twentieth-century debates to try to find out how the category "reason" had come to be educated women's (including feminists') captor via their defensive and strategic participation in academic discourse about knowledge. In one strand of their debates, reason was rejected as an exclusively male characteristic; the body and reproduction were claimed as the source of women's relation to education, knowledge, and service to the world. At the other extreme, women claimed to be equally rational when compared with men. Thus reason, the standard of male superiority, would be the means to their legitimate entry into higher education, and the body would be denied. In either case, "educated woman" as a social category and personal identity became subordinated to "rational man." Educated women succeeded in gaining entry into the previously male-dominated territory of academia; the educated woman, however, was (is) still the "Other of Reason" (Martusewicz, 1988).

I think I'm right about that entrapment in social and academic discourse; it still makes me angry. I experience it firsthand every day as a woman professor in a traditionally feminized field. It's important to try to understand the historical intersection of discourse, knowledge, and identity, and power's weave through them. Make no mistake about it, I am still concerned with the relation between body and mind, but what do we do? Can we write and think about knowledge, or about education, without being in these dualisms? Probably not. I am convinced, in fact, that education does not exist outside this contested space between self and others where the quality of people's lives in relation to each other is at stake. But I'm tired of the anger and wonder if it really leads us anywhere new. It was from this weariness that I began to consider what was going on in other creative aspects of my life that might offer some energy and hope in this struggle.

This essay continues my exploration of the relation between body and mind, but from a very different place. No longer do I write from anger or sadness, nor do I attempt to deny or sublate these responses to very real problems of social injustice. Rather, I write now to try to touch upon and tune into the moving creative process (spirit) that I am convinced is our only hope in finding passage toward different forms of living. I write to try to give a name to something joyous and creative and sensual that moves in the space between body and mind, in spite of the paralyzing effects of Western discourse on the subject.

This writing is a risk, probably the first real risk I've ever taken as a writer in education. But which is riskier, to stay home or to try to write the "something else" that I have no words for, to plunge into uncertain waters? The world needs something more than my anger. Just for a moment I want to search for something else to say. I gather courage from the words of Gilles Deleuze:

We live in a world which is generally disagreeable, where not only people but the established powers have a stake in transmitting sad affects to us. Sadness and its affects are all those which reduce our power to act. The established powers need our sadness to make us slaves. The tyrant, the priest, the captors of souls need to persuade us that life is hard and a burden. . . . In vain someone says, "Let's dance"; we're not really very happy. . . .

It is not easy to be a free man, to flee the plague, organize encounters, increase the power to act, to be moved by joy, to multiply the effects which express or encompass a maximum of affirmation. To make the body a power which is not reducible to an organism, to make thought a power which is not reducible to consciousness. . . . Teaching the soul to live its life, not save it. (Deleuze & Parnet, 1987, p. 61–62)

And so my question is this: Is there a passage here, between body and mind, out of such sad effects and toward the joy of the dance?

Two Writings

During the winters of 1987 and 1988, while I was writing my dissertation and teaching high school social studies and Spanish, I was also teaching young kids to skate. I had about 25 private students ages 5–17, all of whom competed in local competitions. My life during those winters seemed woven together by the snowy car drive from my house to the school where I worked, then to the rink, and back to the study where my dissertation awaited. I spent hours in that little room pondering Foucault, Irigaray, and nineteenth-century women's voices, in my living room piecing together music and choreographing programs (figure skating dances), and on the ice playing between those texts—my dissertation, the music, and my students' bodies. I remember the intensity of this time well.

Sometimes I'd be in my study working with certain texts, and the intensity of the ideas would literally well up in me. Reading those words, trying to make sense of the ideas, and experiencing the thrill of the ideas, I'd feel my body begin to tremble. That's when I'd turn to choreography. I'd get to the point with the concepts I was working with where I simply couldn't sit still. And yet I still needed to say something. It pulsed in me, and so I'd run down the stairs and turn on the music to begin to work on a piece of choreography.

What was happening while I was writing between these very different forms? Why did I run between those writings? What pushed and pulled at me in the composition of those texts, making itself felt, impossible to ignore? And what could we learn about pedagogy in the relation that was created between them?

I am interested in understanding the ways that we are moved to create as teachers, as dancers, as writers, as students. I want to explore the unpredictable effects of that movement, the affirmative power, the excessive relational force that pulses through these endeavors creating unforeseen pathways. In Chapter 1, I introduced Michel Serres' concept of the third man. Serres has written a great deal about what happens when we try to communicate. Drawing from Aristotle's notion of the excluded third man to look at dialogue, Serres shows that in order to communicate we must try to exclude the noise, or the excess information, to get across what we want to say: "the attempt to eliminate noise, is at the same time the condition of the apprehension of the form and the condition of the success of communication" (1982, p. 68). When we say we have understood something, we have recognized some form out of the noise; we have succeeded in excluding the third, that is, in eliminating the "excess empirical." Or so we think.

Actually, we have succeeded in forgetting that the third is there. Writing to form concepts is an active forgetting of the body. The more rigorous one tries to be with the concepts, that is, the more one tries to tighten up the slack of possible interpretations, the more the émpirical is eliminated, the more the body is excluded. Perhaps I was failing in this process; I certainly stopped writing my dissertation in those moments.

In looking for the concepts that would help me to understand those nineteenth-century women, I had to try to exclude my body. I was fighting to know something about reason. But, at the same time, the philosophical texts that I was reading and working with to write the analysis (mostly Michel Foucault, but also Helene Cixous, Luce Irigaray, and other French feminist writing) were very powerful seducers of my body. I mean I felt strong sensual pleasure in reading those texts; the effects of those words danced on my skin. So there was a kind of double dynamic going on: I was fighting to understand and to form concepts as I was reading very moving works. They touched me deeply and welled up in my throat. Often it got to be too much, and then I'd run to the music, as though I was running for my life, running to be alive in choreography.

And now? In my desire to be with music and to choreograph as I write this chapter? Two writings literally struggle for attention. The words come too fast, something is dancing in my body, pushing for attention; I can't stay with the words; choreography is coming.[1]

Choreography

Webster's dictionary says that choreography is "the art of symbolically representing dancing; the composition and arrangement of dances . . . ; a composition created by this art." The Oxford definition is similar: "The written notation of dancing . . . ; the art of representing dancing by signs as singing is by notes."

I would say that it is the art of assembling body moves and gestures to create a dance. It is not necessarily written as a graphic form, but rather as a bodily form. I sometimes record on paper an abbreviation of the sequence of moves, but the actual writing of the program is done with the body, my body and the body of the skater, so that the "sign" is a bodily form. The program becomes, through a kind of stammering between the skater and me, an assemblage of signs made through body gestures and moves.

Several things come to mind here. Choreography is always for me like trying to write in a foreign language. The set of possible signs to be drawn upon are always limited to a particular skater's technical and artistic skills and my understanding of these. That is, as in writing in another language, the strength or weakness of what I communicate through the choreography depends upon my understanding of that collection of signs and my ability to use them (my own knowledge of skating and my ability to play with bodily forms). No matter how large or small the collection of signs, and no matter how strong my knowledge of skating, I am forced to struggle for a form within my understanding of the limits of the other's body. That means there's always the risk that the choreography will fail because I don't yet have a good enough command of the skater's sign system, her technical skills and qualities as a performer. At the same time, I can never know absolutely what those skills and qualities are. So, I stammer.

The stammering is a result of my struggle to say something with another body, even though I can never really control the results. There is always the risk that the skater won't be able to do what the choreography demands. Since the writing itself depends on the skater's body for its signs, if the body is incapable of the positions needed by the developing form, the form fails. And, yet, that space between the writing and the body is also the very condition for what gets created. It is, moreover, the condition of the excitement and joy, and the possibility to be moved. Pedagogy is surfacing.

Writing, Performance, Form

The performance of a piece of choreography is neither different from nor reducible to the choreography itself. I have tried to describe briefly above how the choreography, as a process of writing, is dependent upon the performance. The writing itself is a kind of performance, the success of which depends in part upon the skater's skills with her own body, her ability to perform the moves. That these moves become an assemblage that hangs together is indicative of some degree of success in this respect. But is the performance ever really the same as the choreography? At the same time that the writing depends on the performance to create a form, the form is never the same as the choreography. How is it possible that it is not different and yet not the same? A paradox of difference is operating here.

Let's assume that all the necessary skills are there. What happens as the skater—specifically, Erin, my 11-year-old student and friend—takes the assemblage of moves to her body? The dance, her performance, contests the authorship of the choreography precisely because of what she does as she takes up the gestures. Is it my choreography, my dance, when Erin begins to skate it? Is it even hers?[2] These questions are important if we are to explore and understand the transformative process alive in such creative processes, even those with strict and rigorous demands for a particular form.

What is really exciting is not in the choreography itself or even in the performance, but in what happens *between* them. For while I may have had a specific idea in mind and worked hard to define that idea within the set of gestures and moves, the very relation between my idea and Erin's enactment of it vibrates with the power of difference. Once complete as a text, the piece of choreography can be understood as a set series of moves, or an assemblage abstracted from the skater's body. As soon as the skater takes those moves to herself, however, there is variance, precisely because of the relation. Going back to Serres, there is noise; I'll call it *choreophony* (body noise), which is nothing but the body itself. Let's look more closely at that.

The skater works, works, works to perfect the program, to "get the moves right," to get rid of the noise in the form. Soon the variance is reduced, in an inverse relation with the number of repetitions of each move. Or is it? The skater is perfecting the moves and learning the choreography according to the demands and limits imposed by my notion of the form. But watch a skater practice a program; is the choreophony gone? No! It has simply shifted! There is choreophony or variance in the form, in the movement of the body toward what has been choreographed, even when executed "perfectly," (which I'm convinced is, strictly speaking, impossible, since a perfect performance would mean there is no choreography). Even though the choreography itself has not changed, there is—and will be with each new performance—variance in the form, even in the most rigorous performance.[3] And this is because of the generative force of difference operating in the space between the choreography (constructed in my mind) and the performance (executed with Erin's body).

Or perhaps the choreography, like Erin's body, is what Deleuze calls a "flexion" (1990, p. 285). Perhaps it becomes a kind of body through Erin's body. Perhaps it originated in/as my body. It shifts, and moves, and stretches. And the resulting form, the performed dance or program, is necessarily determined by what happens between these two moving bodies. Each time the skater performs the moves, she repeats what I have written, but at the same moment that she repeats, there is necessarily a difference in the same move. So at the very moment that the choreography is being perfected, it is becoming something else. It both is and is not the choreography; it both is and is not my body. And this is due to the internal dynamic of difference in the relation between the form and its performance.

There is at once in the space between the choreography and its performance, a "suspended gesture" and its virtual performance (Deleuze, 1990, p. 285). Each performance becomes a completed form, necessarily a "simulacrum" in Deleuze's sense, with another suspended form and its performance waiting in the wings, in the space between the form and its repetition.

These two series, the "suspended gesture" and its virtual performance, produce the paradox of movement in the form that challenges Identity, challenges the economy of the Same (Irigaray, 1985). Multiplicity is authenticated in this movement, in the movement of bodies, in the repetition.[4] As Erin claims the form to herself, it is no longer my choreography at all, and not even her dance, once performed; the form moves immediately in an infinite displacement. Without this middle, this space of absolute difference (Derrida's "*differánce*") between the choreography and the performances, there would be no new forms. And because of it, there will never be a stable form. The relational space creates a generative force, disrupts the Identical, causes rupture and movement, and ensures the creation of other forms.

I'm talking about a process of differentiation, a generative force that results when we, as human beings, bring language to the disorder, to the body, when we try to say something about the world and our sensual bodily existence in it. This is what creates that "something else" that moves us, and allows for aesthetic and spiritual experiences of all kinds.

> In language—at the heart of language—the mind grasps the body, and the gestures of the body, as the object of a fundamental repetition. Difference gives things to be seen and multiplies bodies; but it is repetition which offers things to be spoken, authenticates the multiple, and makes of it a spiritual event. (Deleuze, 1990, p. 289)

I'm certain the space in the middle is the source of my excitement and joy in choreography and teaching too. It is what constitutes both the aesthetic and the educational experience. I'm sure that the series of spaces between the writing of my dissertation and the choreography, between the ice, the study, and living room floor, between Erin and me, between the choreography and the performance all played together in the creation of these texts. And I'm sure this creative movement is why I'm in education. But is it simply the production of difference that is important here? Let's go back to the ice.

Difference and Judgment

In every repeated form, different choreophony emerges. Or maybe we could say that every form is created out of this empirical choreophony, which is never completely absent from the completed form. We are merely ignoring, excluding, refusing to see the "excess" body moves, the flex, when we say that the skater is learning the program. And when we watch the performance as the choreographer, coach, or spectator, we judge that choreophony to be something beautiful or exciting. Or we judge it to be a mistake, depending upon any number of contextually driven criteria. This judgment is not derived from any *a priori* set of absolute rules, but rather from a particular historically effected set of circumstances and expectations. Many people feel frustrated or perplexed sometimes by such judgment when watching world-class figure skating competitions on television. I certainly have heard myself exclaim, "How could those judges mark her down? That was beautiful!"

Imagine what might emerge there on the ice, if the skater played with each variation that was judged beautiful, even by herself. The form that would eventually emerge if such play were allowed—and after many repetitions—would not be identifiable with the original choreography (see Daignault, 1983). We know that such play with the piece is seldom allowed to happen for any number of reasons—not the least important of which is the choreographer's ego and "possession" of the piece—but especially because an attention to collective interpretations of beauty is likely to be operating. That is, there are always both personal desires operating and an associated context of normative standards of beauty and accuracy that influence what forms are allowed or intended to emerge. I will discuss the ways that desire is shaped within these relations and can negatively impact the creative process in Chapters 4 and 5. Normative standards, of course, can be exclusive to the point of violence, not just in artistic forms but also in all kinds of social relational endeavors, including the creation of communities, for example. And yet, not to judge would leave us with nihilism, the belief that any form, practice, or belief is as beautiful or good as the next.

For Erin and me, there was usually a rather wonderful give-and-take, a sort of collaborative effort and understanding as we went through this creative process. I deeply respected her ability to interpret my initial choreography. She did so willingly, often with abandon because she respected my desire to create and she listened carefully to what I was trying to communicate. This, of course, was not always the case, and sometimes in my desire to "get the piece right," to refine her choreophony, she'd get resistant or frustrated, and there would be conflict. This is to be expected when judgment and the exclusion of "noise" is the task at hand.

To create a dance through choreography, like other forms of communication, is to try to exclude the "excess empirical," and what gets defined as excess is usually the prerogative of the choreographer whose goal is, after all, to say something. But as Serres writes, "to exclude the empirical is to exclude differentiation" (1982, p. 69). This is the position we are forced to accept when we judge anything. We decide between what is the "real" or "good" or "beautiful" form and what is merely choreophony. If we want a form, if we want to create a dance, such judgment and the exclusion of what we deem to be undesirable is inevitable.

Unfortunately, such judgment too often ignores or is blind to the undecidability between the variation and the form, and insists that a "true" form (i.e., a form true to the "real" choreography) exists outside of the variation. When we say we have excluded all the empirical variation (all that unnecessary meaning, all those unnecessary voices), we claim to know and thus claim the right to judge. We may assume a kind of universal truth. That's how the body (and fantasy) gets excluded by knowledge. It's reason's game. This is precisely the kind of exclusionary practice that I wrote about while a graduate student, and that my dissertation was dedicated to understanding. Spurred on by a concept of reason put forth by the Enlightenment philosophes as a capacity possessed in more developed form or even exclusively by some and not by others, this practice of judgment relies on a concept of truth as universally given, foundational and thus discoverable by those with the capacity to "know." The violence of this game in endeavors we call "educational" is familiar, but is it necessary?

How do we avoid it? Isn't thinking itself implicated in this problematic? Given the violence implied, "how do we save the honor of thinking"—or teaching, or choreographing?[5] This is the crux of aesthetic and ethical problematics of all kinds. We are forced to evaluate, to judge, and in so doing something necessarily gets denied, excluded, and sometimes the results are harmful.

Too often throughout history we have assumed that in such exclusion we could get to the truth, to what is real, to the true form, the choreography itself. And if we want to say something, to communicate, or to create something, we have to try. I am aware of the operation of this power to judge as I think about my relation to Erin. I think of all the potential that was there while we worked together; I think of all the possibility encapsulated within her ability to express things with her body, forms and gestures that I can but imagine. And yet, working with her to create a particular form, many of those possibilities got pushed back—both by my demands and by her own understanding and desire to create something within the bounds of normative expectations—in order for others to emerge. One could easily imagine that the demands of the choreographer could indeed create a kind of violence to the skater's sensibilities. Because I had a deep respect for her talent and her desire to create, our relationship was much more collaborative than many such relationships might be; I truly depended on her interpretive ability to translate what I was trying to say, and we were both constantly working to exclude "the noise." In spite of our efforts, however, all that virtuality was always present there in the wings, in the relation between my idea, her movement, and her potential movement; and when a bit of that potential emerged unexpectedly, I was sometimes dismayed and often blown away by its aesthetic force.

What I'm arguing here is that there is a difficult and complicated set of experiences created by this generative force. If we want to create something, we must accept the responsibility of choosing between all the differences that get created in the interpretive spaces of our (pedagogical) relations with each other. Such choosing holds the danger of violence within it, and yet the forms we create out of these necessary choices will never remain stable. The so-called true form is, strictly speaking, impossible. A simulacrum is always at play, undermining truth as identity. The choreographer (or the teacher, or the statesperson) is only under an illusion of possession—the space between the idea and its performance sees to that. The force of differentiation dances on the page or across the stage. Something moves in spite of the power of the illusion, making it possible to question exclusion and to make attempts to remedy injustice. What moves there?

To Be Moved

I am often deeply touched by a skater's performance. I feel a welling up in my throat, a tingle on my skin. What moves me to cry when I watch Erin perform the choreography (or when I read a student's work)? Certainly, I'm proud that she has accomplished the form. Marx has taught us a lot about the importance of our relation to the product of our labor, and to be human is precisely about this relation. But it's not my self that I find there in that form, not at all. In fact, I often experience a confusing sense of dismay simultaneously with a rush of exhilaration. The form is not what I sought or thought, though it may be very moving. To be moved means to be touched by this paradoxical differential force. Deleuze explains that "personal uncertainty is not a doubt foreign to what is happening, but rather an objective structure of the event itself, insofar as it moves in two directions at once, and insofar as it fragments the subject following this double direction" (1990, p. 3).

This realization is what the so-called postmodern crisis of representation is about. The subject or self is not there in the dance or in the writing, but surely it is not dead. It is movement itself, in language and on the body. That is, our sense of self comes through our attempts to say something about who we are and what we feel, to capture those moments, and it comes through our actual sensual experiences of the world. But what we are experiencing never sits still; what we are experiencing is nothing more or less than pure movement of difference, a pure becoming in Deleuze's terms.

Such an affirmation of becoming is thus an affirmation of hope for different ways of living. As I indicated above, this affirmative movement depends upon our active engagement, our decisions, our judgments, our choices between this gesture, this word, this idea and that. This is the source of the possibility for justice, for an ethical orientation to the world, and for an emancipatory politics that does not depend upon foundational or *a priori* notions of truth. For now, however, I want to get a closer look at the affirmative movement that is at the heart of this possibility.

As a choreographer and as a teacher, I often experience this affirmative sense as joy, a welling up of pleasure in my chest and throat. Sometimes I cry, often I gasp or laugh for the sheer amazement of what gets made, or for the momentary recognition of the creative process playing on me.

The production of a form through choreography is autoerotic. By this I mean that when I write choreography I am aware that I am writing pleasure for myself. I am writing on my body and on the body of someone else a form that is not really mine. Inspiring words by Helene Cixous come to mind: "Write yourself. Your body must be heard" (1981, p. 250). Put yourself into the text and into your classroom. And then I hear Deleuze and Parnet: "One has to lose . . . one's face in it" (1987, p. 45). Choreography is not about writing myself, but it is about writing on and with and about my body—making my body heard and felt, but as a process of losing myself, of becoming something else, something I don't really know. I don't think "who am I?" as I choreograph. Something gets made, but *I* am not at its center; *I* am not its source.

In the process of the making of the piece, in its performances, intensities rain down, well up, make me cry. Agony and pleasure. What is that? More than the movement of an unstable form. More than the form. The Stoics called it *extra-being*,[6] the something between the choreography and the form. To be moved by a piece of skating is an effect of the proliferation of difference between the choreography and the performance. It is to be touched by the difference, the intensity. The condition for the movement, the space between, is also the condition of being moved by the piece. I mean it is the condition of our response to the piece, the condition for the aesthetic existence of the piece: movement to be moved.

"To move" and "to be moved" are the effects of bodies. Movement across a cold, hard surface, skidding, leaping, stammering, spinning, moving. "Move, Erin!" She does and I'm touched; and the "to move" and "to be moved" fling out like a throw of the dice. Nonexisting entities, effects of these bodies, effects of this repetition, traces of effects. Something moves there.

So many movements! The moves of the choreography, Erin's body, the form, something down my spine, something that resists my *knowing*. All of this movement gets made within the paradoxical space of choreography and performance: a wonderful bouquet of bodies, movement, and time! Let's take a closer look at this with the help of Deleuze's reading of the Stoics.

Deleuze uses the concept of effect to try to describe, much as a physicist might, the invisible, immaterial particles that result from the fact that we use language and other symbolic forms. These immaterial particles produce events that are thus meaningful. Effects and events are expressed or described with the use of infinitives. Thus, when we say "to be moved" we are not talking about something that *exists* as a body, or even as a state of affairs. But it does depend on bodies and it does do something. We are talking about an incorporeal effect that *subsists*, an effect of the relation between bodies, or an effect of an effect. The "to move" and "to be moved" are effects produced within relations between bodies, passions, actions, gestures, all sorts of assemblages.

An *assemblage* is a mixture or composition of bodies: bodies in bodies, movements in bodies, passions and actions in bodies. "To be moved" is an effect of an assemblage—a dance, a class, a piece of writing. And the signs that make up the assemblage—the body gestures, the moves, the words— could be traces of other effects; that is they could be traces of effects made from other assemblages. To be moved by an assemblage, then, could be to be touched by the effects of such traces. I am quite certain this was the event I was experiencing as I ran down the stairs from the words of Foucault to turn on the music and compose a piece of choreography.

To say that "to be moved" does not exist is not to say that it does not affect us. It simply means it is incorporeal. We cannot see it or touch it, but it touches us. Like a phantasm, it pushes its way to the surface and gets caught in our throats. It sits there insisting on being recognized by our senses, our skin, our stomachs, and our minds. Foucault has used the phrase "incorporeal materiality" (1977, p. 169) to capture what Deleuze is getting at.

As an incorporeal effect, "to be moved" does not exist in an visible sense. It subsists between the signs or symbolic forms that we use to make sense of the world, but cannot be reduced to the signs themselves, or even to the signifying system. Or perhaps better, the system cannot simply be reduced to signs, to the movement of signifiers and signifieds; something else moves in the spaces between.

Moving Between Dissertation and Choreography and . . .

"To move, to be moved": the infinitive is important, there is no subject present, no *I*; *it* moves, something moves as the effect of an assemblage, or as the effect of other effects. I think back to the dissertation and all those chore-ographies. What moved me? What made me run to the music: effects found as traces in the signs of those texts? I could not write those effects, that danc-ing on my skin, that thumping in my chest into the dissertation. The form of the work forbade it. So, I ran for the music, for my body, and my students' bodies. I ran for the ice, where a form awaited that would take the rushing effects of those other texts.

But what got written? Was I displacing the traces of curriculum theory or French philosophy into the dance? Were Irigaray and Deleuze dancing as effects on that ice surface? Not the people, nor their names, nor even the names of their names, but the traces of effects of their works and their words on my body, and hence on Erin's too. Was the dance created through traces of those effects, displaced and re-created as the signs of the body? And then what? I went back to the dissertation. What effects from the ice and my stu-dents' bodies got written there? Did the effects of the choreography that moved me, move into that text? It's difficult to know, but let's look at that.

Let's hypothesize that in choreography, the body is used (at least in part, and not necessarily consciously) to write signs that are traces of effects and intensities playing in the choreographer's life. The repetition and difference that take place between the writing and the performance produce different effects and intensities; the performance of those signs, therefore, is a repeti-tion of effects that produces different effects. Choreography, in this sense, becomes writing with the body that which plays on the body; writing with the body to be moved. An interesting series emerges: to be moved to write to be moved . . . to write . . .

And what of this writing, here on this page? I am writing about choreog-raphy and performance. This writing makes of the body and its gestures (which write a repetition of, and therefore make an object of, the incorporeal within the dance), the object of another repetition. If choreography somehow takes as its object the incorporeal (the effects of texts that rain down on me), this writing must be the repetition of a repetition of the incorporeal. Within the repetition of the repetition, difference and differences of intensity move, pro-ducing multiplicity, dissolving me.[7]

In and between each series the space between the mind and the body produces movement through differentiation, and this plays on the body sen-sually. I feel it. This writing is playing with the two series and the spaces of difference operating both within and between them. It is precisely within that play of differentiation, between the body and the mind, that we are moved. It is precisely within those spaces of differentiation that language moves. It is precisely between the movement of language and the intensity "to be moved" that pedagogy does its creative affirmative work.

In the spaces of relation, *differánce*, and differentiation, the movement of language and the "to be moved" threaten the empire of Identity. And the subject of pedagogy (Daignault, 1989) dances joyously away, affirming life itself.

Pedagogy and Education

As I write this, revisiting the joy of my work as a choreographer, I am very aware that my work as a teacher educator has come close to this. As I have said in earlier chapters, I often experience, as I'm sure most teachers do, great rushes of passion and sensuality while listening to my students or reading their work. I have become aware that there are all sorts of transformations going on for all of us as we struggle together to think about the complex forces that affect teachers and students in schools. And I am aware, too, that each of us brings into our relation with each other effects from all sorts of other texts that dance across the pedagogical spaces there in the classroom. In much the same way that I was aware of Erin's incredible potential, I feel the force of all sorts of unconscious, unintended effects brought into that space by my students as I interact with them. I'm certain that these effects are part of what creates the unpredictable questions and beautiful ideas that touch and move me.

But is it enough to revel in these differences? While pedagogy clearly enacts the paradoxical relation between performance and form, undermining the identity of ideas and foundational truth in much the same way as choreography and dance do, like the choreographer and the dancer, both the teacher and students must learn to choose or the form will fail. In the case of teaching, the choice often involves questions of the good. Just as the dance demands the question, What is the beautiful form? education insists that we ask, How are we to live?

"To be moved" by the skater or my students is created neither in the indifference of nihilistic pleasure or the violence of universal notions of truth. The joy of both these endeavors is generated precisely because something incredible gets made as we choose between forms in the choreography and again in the performance, or in the decision of what to teach and again for the student as they listen and create responses. With each repeated choice new possibilities open up, and new differences—some that may cause conflict—dance between us. How do we teach in the face of such possibilities and the ensuing choices?

This is not a simple process. There is always the danger that when we create something—a dance, a text, a course—we try too hard to control the process with our decisions, our authority; or, alternatively, we avoid the necessity to judge. In either case, the form we create will fail. And, as I explore in the next two chapters, there are all kinds of desires created within the contexts where teachers and students meet that can influence the generative process and interfere with our critical capacities to choose well. This is the dilemma that the creative process demands we face collectively.

And something moves.

Notes

1. When I wrote this chapter, I also wrote a piece of choreography with Erin Vieau, this time intentionally working between the two texts to compose companion pieces. I presented a videotape of my student's performance of the piece when I presented the paper at Bergamo. That tape is available from me for anyone interested.

2. There are echoes here of Yeats' famous line, "Who can tell the dancer from the dance?"

3. No doubt this part of my analysis will sound familiar to those who have read or heard Jacques Daignault's work. I am indebted to him for the thinking that created and was created in this paper (see specifically Daignault, 1983). Daignault's work led me to the work of his predecessor Gilles Deleuze (see Deleuze, 1990).

4. Deleuze writes:

This . . . paradoxical entity circulates in both series and for this reason assures their communication. It is a two sided entity, equally present in the signifying and signified series. It is the mirror. Thus, it is at once word and thing, name and object, sense and denotatum, expression and designation, etc. It guarantees therefore the convergence of the two series which it traverses, but precisely on the condition that it make them diverge. (1990, p. 40)

5. I am paraphrasing Jean François Lyotard here who states as a problem the following: "Given 1) the impossibility of avoiding conflicts (the impossibility of indifference) and 2) the absence of a universal genre of discourse to regulate them (or, if you prefer, the inevitable partiality of the judge): to find, if not what can legitimate judgment (the "good" linkage), then at least how to save the honor of thinking" (1988, p. xii).

6. Deleuze has written extensively on the work of the Stoics. This analysis draws on his work (1990).

7. All of this draws directly on Deleuze's reading of the Stoics and his analysis of repetition and difference as laid out in *The Logic of Sense* (1990).

Chapter 4

Say Me to Me

Desire and Education

What is love's knowledge, and what writing does it dictate in the heart?

—Martha C. Nussbaum

I know that little girl's passion for questions. The pleasure of the questions. Warm sun on her back. Looking at grass. "Why do I see green? Does my mother see the same green, or is her green blue, like my sky? Does this sky touch me?" Something moves her. There's a limit here; she knows she can't know the answers, and yet . . . something else touches her. I feel her desire to share these questions, for someone else to feel the intensity, the wonder of it all. And perhaps to be touched by another's wonder too, a desire for connection to the world and to the other, through this passion to know.

She runs into the kitchen. She runs in there with her questions. "Mom! Could your green be my blue? What is the sky?" She gives them to her. She wants her to love them too, to love her questions. At four she knows that love is in those questions, a particular kind of love. It's impossible that her mother should not know this. But the woman does not turn; she remains at the sink.

I'm not sure this scene ever really happened or if I have created it out of some vague and lingering confusion, where the joy of thinking about the world and its mysteries, mingles with a sense of disappointment. It is a disappointment connected at once to this wonder about the world, a sense of caring, and love for the unknown, and to a strong desire to be loved myself, loved for my questions, for me. Two kinds of love and desire intertwine, one a strong love of the world, a desire to know it, to think and to understand and thus to be connected; the other, a desire to be loved or affirmed *because* I want to know this world. Throughout my life, I have felt the collision of these two forms in a variety of contexts: my mother's kitchen, an academic conference, and even now as I write.

I have felt the rush of creation that comes in the wake of asking a particular question. And I have felt the disappointment of not getting it right or, more accurately, of not getting back what I wanted, and the burgeoning violence that this latter desire invites. A violent disappointment seeps in, pulls me down, stops the questions and the joy. I think that this experience is not uncommon and that looking at it carefully could teach us much about what comes to interfere with education. There are violent forms of desire associated with our egos that come to shut down our willingness to be open to a different desire, the desire for the unknown. In this chapter I will look at how the desire for affirmation can be an obstacle to our willingness to be in the generative pedagogical process and thus ultimately to education.

Culture and Desire

"It is always something bad to injure one's own power of thought, since thought is the condition of all that is good."

—Simone Weil

I use the word *violent* here because the strength of the disappointment when I don't get back what I hope for can kill the creative process (which I will argue for as part of the educational process) and become harmful both to me and to others. It is a trap, and it shuts down thought, which can only be harmful.

I begin from the premise that the forces shaping forms of desire "are the cultural codes and representations which derive from the historical and collective relations between men and women" (Brenkman, 1993, p. 64). Desire, in all its forms, said or unsaid, is culturally learned and maintained through the very generative processes I have been describing. Certain forms of desire are at the crux of the perpetuation of social and psychic violence, as well as violence to the Earth and to other sentient and nonsentient beings.

Yet, there is also a kind of desire that motivates our struggles against domination and toward a connection with others, toward interbeing and justice. I do not mean desire as a transcendental force, but rather individually experienced desire generated out of and through our relation to each other and to the Earth and its creatures that motivates and is generated within the struggle to care for each other. Desire for a better world, for justice, and for truth generates questions and pushes us to challenge forms of social injustice by offering new ways of thinking and being.

This essay will explore this contradictory relation, the points at which the desire for affirmation, praise, or recognition overtakes the desire for truth, justice, or understanding, stopping the questions and ultimately the joy that makes education possible. What is this desire for affirmation (sometimes misunderstood as love) and why does it too often turn so heavy? What are the particular contexts and political relations within which such disappointment and the accompanying possibility of self-negation are generated? What are the effects of these negative effects of desire for education and for the possibility of new thoughts for the world?

These are clearly ethical and aesthetic questions. I approach these questions here autobiographically, not only reflecting on my own particular life and the broader culture in which I live but also exploring how one should live in this culture. It is this very commitment that pushes me to teach, to ask questions, and to encourage my students to ask their own questions that will open pathways for thinking.

My concern in this chapter is with a particular and, I think, too common danger that lies in the path of this endeavor. Specifically, I want to explore how the violent effects of certain forms of desire turn us away from the conditions necessary for education.

Questions

I'll begin with some thoughts about questions. What is it to ask a question? To ask is always a repetition, a repetition of the why or the how, for example, as the play between what we know and don't know, between the thought and the unthought, and always between the said and the unsaid. As such, a question is an invitation to the play of multiplicity that operates between the given and the virtual, as between self and other. I mean that when we ask why, when we repeat that linguistic function, we are opening a *space* in which there are an indefinite number of possible answers for us to choose, some more interesting and some more accurate or sensible than others.

I'm convinced that this space between our questions and all the possible answers, a space of pure difference, is where the possibility and the thrill of teaching come from. This space is a pedagogical space; its indefinite creation is precisely what allows and ensures different possibilities to spring forth. For as we attempt to answer why and to choose the best solution, still another set of whys come, and the space of possibility—never separate from and yet irreducible to our attempts to say something—is opened once again, and again, indefinitely. Gilles Deleuze puts it this way:

just as solutions do not suppress problems, but on the contrary discover in them the subsisting conditions without which they would have no sense, nor do they saturate the question, which persists in all the answers. There is therefore an aspect in which problems remain without a solution, and therefore without an answer. It is in this sense that problem and question . . . have their own being. (1990, p. 56)

This space of question and solution is the boundary between the world and our attempts to comment on it, or make sense of it. It is at once a limit and an empty space, forming the condition for both what has been said and what is to come. And though I have said that it was the questions that made me run to the kitchen, it is actually this limit space that generates for me the sense of awe and joy in trying to think.

As I wrote in the previous chapter, this relational space is what generates the wonder at all those possibilities for beauty. It also generates the possibilities for understanding myself and others in this world, for loving this world. That sense fuels my life. This is why I so joyfully ran. And this is why I teach.

To teach (perhaps especially to teach teachers) is to share with others the exhilaration and the difficulties of opening oneself (and others) onto this limit space, of stepping out to a precipice and confronting the unthought. To be there in that process of repetition and difference is to be in the midst of pedagogy and to feel alive in the affirmative life force that courses through that space.

That was what I discovered in the grass, that I could ask a question and recognize the essential limitations of finding an answer while still experiencing the desire to know. This joyous recognition of the simultaneous fullness and limitation of this space was what I was so excited about sharing with my mother. It is just this infinite pedagogical fullness that is the source of all transformative possibility and thus of hope that the world could be better.

So then, what is the problem? (Yet another question!) Where does the disappointment come from, and more important, what can it do? What is its violence?

To ask a question is always to want something. In the scene I shared at the beginning of the paper, I ran to my mother with my questions because I had been touched by something. A recognition of the limit space had brushed me. I ran because I wanted to share a sudden understanding that as humans we have a capacity for perceiving and searching for truth, for thinking about our connections to larger life processes. This capacity, however, is limited by the very function that allows us to think—our power to name the sky blue or the grass green. I ran for the sheer joy of that truth.

I also ran for myself. This is important, for there is an intensity of aspiration in the asking of those questions, aspiration for the world and aspiration for myself.

In Search of Recognition: Say Me to Me

Part of the desire that pushes me to ask about this world, that pushes me to that precipice, is a desire to understand myself in this world. That is, there is the desire (and the anxiety) to know who I am and to recognize myself in the face of others. I look for others to say, "Ah yes, I know what you mean. I recognize you." And this is so when I write, or teach, or choreograph. I push my thinking and my questions out in search for a truth that will connect me to the world.

This is the desire for the unthought, for an unsaid and unknown other to recognize and so affirm me, to "say me to me."[1] But the unthought, the limit space does not give me "me." It gives me nothing, which is to say everything: the questions come flooding in and with them all the possibilities of who I might be and what this world might be. And so I run to known others—my students, my teachers, my lover, and my mother. I give them my questions and I search for myself in their responses. And this is where the potential problem lies, for the others in my life cannot give "me" to me. I may search for myself out there, but the "me" that I seek is always already other than the "me" they may reflect back. And this is because of the supplementary process alive in all interpretive relations and in all question posing.

I cannot separate myself, me, from the aspiration to ask or from the exhilaration of facing the unthought. The "me" is simultaneously there on the edge with the question and out there in the virtual, in the unthought. Our sense of self, the "me," is never disconnected from the infinite movement of thought, questions, and meaning making. Any recognition of "me" will simply be reinterpreted and recast in an ongoing translational process. And so there is no "me" except to the extent that I exist in the other that is always just ahead on the nomadic field of meaning making.

To get caught in a desire for the "me" is a prelude to violence, because to give those questions in the illusion of a return of myself, is to forget, or deny, difference. The desire for the "me" is inescapable, but the "me" is, strictly speaking, unattainable, except to the extent that it is given in "the other of the me" itself or in the questions and creative possibilities that are generated in the thought about the world. Jacques Derrida deals with this writing:

> When he writes himself to himself, he writes himself to the other who is infinitely far away. . . . He has no relation to himself that is not forced to defer itself by passing through the other. . . . (1985b, p. 88)

In our teaching, our writing, our loving, we search for others who will affirm our lives and share our aspirations and our questions, who will care that we are alive and help to connect the "me" to the world. And yet, this "me" is inevitably tied to those questions I keep mentioning, to the limit space and the desire to transcend the limitations of our ability to find answers. Again, the questions tie "me" to the other. The questions are "me" and other, tied to this Earth, to the ones I love, and to my limited time here. But they also mark what I do not know, what is not yet thought, the indefinite movement of difference in identity and in knowledge.

Tied to a "me" that does not yet exist, the questions are always different and deferred as soon as they appear. The danger lies in the experience of this difference as a failure, either to fulfill or to be fulfilled. Such a weighty disappointment can shut down thinking and the play of questions, leading to a kind of terrorism of the soul.

You can see the problem. We search for identity, for connection to the world, and for love, at the same time that we seek transcendence from this imperfect "humanity," this essential emptiness of being. That is a critical existential problem: to desire to be more than human, while we are "all too human." That is, we learn that while we want to know, our knowing is limited by the tools that we have at our disposal, the relation, for example, between our ability to name and to perceive. I learned this in the grass, and I'm learning it again as I read philosophy.

On Desire and the Imperfect

I'm afraid of disappointing you. With the desire to fulfill your expectations comes a specific anxiety, the one whose mimetic nature is only confirmed by overly explicit denials: the anxiety of facing the other.

—René Girard

The first thing we know about ourselves is that we are not perfect. Teaching in the early part of the twentieth century, French philosopher and activist Simone Weil told her students, "The only mark of God in us is that we know we are not God." And yet we are not satisfied with this imperfection; we believe it should not be so, that we should and perhaps could transcend the limit space. "We feel we should not be imperfect and limited; if it were perfectly right and proper to be so then we would not think ourselves imperfect" (Weil, 1979, p. 90).

Our relation to imperfection is the source of both joy and violence. Around this experience of ourselves circulates desire for the truth. It pushes us to problematize ourselves, to ask questions about who we are in the world. Since the imperfection or limitations never go away (though we may push past some limits, others are always on the horizon), neither do the questions. They continue to circulate, as I argued earlier, indefinitely.

This is often quite difficult because the ego is also present in this process. Another desire may manifest itself in the desire to be perfect and to seek the recognition of others. Here desire helped along by the ego may turn toward negative forms of power and the illusion that one has reached or neared the status of God. We don't have to go far for examples: History has given the world its share of despots in politics as well as in philosophy. But such desire for power, recognition, or affirmation is not found only in those extreme cases. The ego operates in all of us. The desire for power over others and the violence it entails is a cultural and psychological monster fed by the belief that we ought not be imperfect.

René Girard's well-known work, *Violence and the Sacred* (1977), helps to illuminate the ways in which violence may follow upon this experience of imperfection. According to Girard, the desire to be affirmed by the other involves the desire for that which we perceive the other to want, and is thus essentially mimetic. Desire in this case is focused on the object of the desire of the other, an object perceived as holding within it "being," and thus the power to deliver the "me." The subject believes that the object of the other's desire holds the key to *her* being; therefore affirmation from the model—the parent, the teacher, the lover—has the effect of deliverance from uncertainty and arrival at being. Such an experience of fullness is of course illusory and easily deflated. Fullness is quickly exchanged for nothingness and disappointment. As Girard teaches us, such shifting positions too often lead to jealousy, rivalry, and the escalation of violence, as disciple and model struggle over who is to be first with the object.

This is the economy of the ego, the plane of exchange, where the reward of affirmation is the currency sought: "Love me. Say it. Say my name." The movement from affirmation to rejection and back to affirmation creates tremendous energy. This is the energy that so fascinated Hegel. Essentially violent, it was, he believed, the basis for transcendence. Perhaps Hegel was writing too close to his own ego; he missed what plays on the body and the heart as one stands on the precipice. He was too fascinated with mind to pay attention to those effects. Referring to Hegel this way, however, is only an expression of my will to power. A story of my own would serve better here.

On Ego and Education: Three Statements

The story that I want to tell is really a series of stories strung together by three statements. It is about both education and ego as each comes to circulate and tease in the pedagogical relation. Tracing this series of events in my own life, moments marked particularly by the bodily experience of the desire for affirmation and its dangerous effects, I will explore the difference between the will to truth (structured by the free play of questions and the generative force of difference) and the will to power (structured by mimetic desire).

The three statements that comprise my story are these: (1)"You have not risked"; (2)"You have arrived"; and (3)"Those were very different papers." These statements form a sort of developmental series, not in the sense of any predetermined ontological or teleological series, but rather as a series made meaningful by the relation that each statement has to the other two. These statements were made and heard separately, in three different years, at the annual JCT Conference on Curriculum Theorizing and Classroom Practice, known informally as the Bergamo conference.

In 1989 I presented a paper that was a piece of my dissertation. It was a sound paper and was fairly well received, but I was unexcited. I said so to a friend, a person with whom I have shared many questions, and who had been a primary teacher and model for me for many years. He responded, "You have not risked. You have presented what you know." What could that mean? I had no idea, but the statement shook me. I felt very uncomfortable. Something was stirring me up. I felt mobilized, moving toward the precipice.

The next year I presented again. The paper was a version of Chapter 3, "Choreography and Curriculum Theory," and was indeed a risk. I had written about the joy of teaching. The words in that paper and their effects had come from my heart, from the knowledge in my body of the joy created as one works hard to say something, to teach something to someone else. I remember feeling very peaceful as I presented, even while my heart was racing. I had danced up to the edge of the limit space. And this time, without any question from me, I heard from my mentor, "You have arrived."

I had indeed "arrived"; I thought I was in heaven as my friends and colleagues praised my work. I certainly was basking in the glow of recognition and affirmation. But I was to discover that this was a most dangerous arrival.

The pragmatic effects of that statement, expressed within a particular context and in a particular set of circumstances as part of a series, sent me into the economy of my ego. This was the reward it had been waiting for, finally to be heard, to have my peers, my colleagues, my teacher say my name: "Rebecca, you have arrived." Operating in the textual relation of this comment and the circumstances of my life—all the old longings, disappointments, and desires—was a powerful "order word." Deleuze and Guattari use this concept to describe incorporeal transformations of bodies that are affected in statements. They argue that "to order, question, promise or affirm is not to inform someone about a command, doubt, engagement or assertion but *to effectuate these specific, immanent and necessarily implicit acts*" (1987, p. 77; emphasis added).

To say "you have arrived" was not to inform me of that event, but to effectuate it, to effectuate a specific, incorporeal, transformative arrival. I don't mean that this transformation was necessarily to a new and better place. And I don't mean that it occurred as a result of any intention of the speaker. It was an arrival incited by the statement's colliding with and fueling a specific kind of desire, a desire for the pleasure of affirmation and the power of recognition.

This pleasure was quite different from that taken in the questions and the writing of the paper. This was a pleasure taken in the power that I felt in the event of recognition, both transported by and not reducible to the words of my teacher. The "being recognized" by my peers and my teacher happened in the transformative power of the order word, as an event. I had instantly taken a new position in the academic game; I had moved upstream (Serres, 1982, pp. 15-17). It felt good to hear my name.

But I was scared too. Defensive. I remember asking, "What if I never write such a paper again?" It was my ego speaking. This statement, made violent by mimetic desire, was taking my heart. The desire for recognition, the energy of the ego, is fueled by the sense of nothingness that the limit space brings. Denying the moment of absolute fullness, the ego rushes in to fill the void. A kind of happiness ensues, a happiness created from a sense of power and control over the void: "I'm something—look at me!" Girard's thesis seems all too clear here.

Truth was and is a powerful object of desire for me, and I must admit that in the presence of this teacher I believed I had access to truth. I felt sure that I had finally found a person who would not disappoint me, but rather a person who would share with me this love of the limit space and grant me the kind of understanding that I had been searching for, someone who would "say me to me."

His words, "you have arrived," meant to me that I had arrived where I believed *he* was, that I had grasped what I believed *he* wanted (a certain knowledge of the limit space and/or ability to express it), and that I had therefore achieved some sort of fullness. His words gave me the "me" my ego had been seeking. Or at least an illusion of me.

Powerful academic woman? But what a dangerous identity to covet! Powerful academic woman propelled up the mountain by a massive ego energy, by the belief that I was no longer empty. It was a temporary gusto, of course. I felt the fear of losing my position, or perhaps it was the fear of the certain danger of that position. For as Michel Serres (1982, pp. 15-28) has so aptly demonstrated, it is when one is in the maximum position that one is most vulnerable to the violence of others. A sense of competition and rivalry settled upon me; and, as always, it too quickly became evident that something was amiss: me.

The year following my success is important. I wrote yet another paper. It was a struggle. I've struggled before; I'm struggling now. Indeed, the work to bring something to life, to create something, is usually difficult, an odd mixture of frustration and exhilaration. But this was different. I felt no joy in it. When I think of that summer, I understand the expression "her heart wasn't in it," but I pressed on, motivated by the previous year's success. When I finally presented, I felt none of the exhilaration of the year before, though there was anxiety. I said so, again to my teacher.

"Those were very different papers," he responded. A fairly innocuous statement on its own, but my heart sank a million miles. That old disappointment was seeping in again: "I'm nothing!" Pain flooded my body. Chained to this very weighty desire, my heart was like a ton of bricks.

At home I wept. And for months afterward I was in the bluest, blackest intellectual and psychological place, unable to think, going through the motions with my students. The sense of fullness was replaced by defeat. In the passage from fullness to nothingness, the whole mimetic process escalated— the disappointment, the anger, the jealousy, the sad passion. René Girard has written of this vertigo, describing the process of instability and alternation that accompanies mimetic desire. In the mimetic structure, the need to be first with the object of desire leads to rivalry and competition between the model and the disciple. Oscillation between victory and defeat escalates the violence in social relations and the need for a sacrifice (1977, pp. 149–150). Girard's analysis of tragedy in Greek mythology shows that this sacrifice is necessary to avoid total destruction in a community and usually involves the selection of a scapegoat. In order to protect the community from the escalation of conflict, scapegoats are sent away in exile or offered up in sacrifice in a symbolic but necessary purging of violence from the community.

In my case, the rivalry that I felt most sharply was not with my mentor (at least not explicitly) but with myself. The violence was not turned upon an outside other, but rather inward upon myself. Rather than engage external conflict, I chose myself first as rival (will I ever write such a paper again?) and later as scapegoat (no, I'm too stupid!). Simone Weil warns against such self-injury. To turn violence upon oneself is ultimately, she tells us, an ethical problem, since it is injurious to thought and thought is the only passage that we have toward a different world (Weil, 1979, p. 196). My ego had shut down the questions.

It's difficult to write about that time. I was afflicted, sick and sad from the wrong passion. I had been headed for this place for a year, maybe two. This was what the arrival had really been about. My pain was, to use a phrase coined by Deleuze and Guattari, "naked, vegetative egoism"(1987, p. 36). Teaching was impossible because I could not turn my attention outward toward the other, toward the questions or the unthought.

I had taken a trip through a writing/thinking process that was quite simply an example of what happens when our attention is not focused on a problem that we sincerely feel. This was not writing as thinking; this was an academic exercise. It failed because it was primarily motivated by the desire for recognition, by self-love and not by love of the truth, not by a concern for the world. The sacrifice that I had imposed on myself was a serious ethical problem precisely because I could not engage thought outward to the world and to the other. The questions stopped; I was not able to open myself to the limit space. I was suffering from what Buddhists call *dhukka*, an ugly, neurotic, ego-bound suffering.

The following spring, still feeling defeated, I considered not going to Bergamo. As May 15, the deadline for proposals, approached, I found myself in a kind of paralysis—throat-constricting, stomach-knotting panic. What was I going to propose? I began to struggle. I had no question, no project, no problematic. Time was closing in. This was impossible! Visions of failure swamped me. This was my conference, my summer writing time. "But I have no problem!"

Of course I did. How is it possible to be so disturbed and not to have a question? How funny: The problem was that I had no problem! Questions flew to the screen of my computer. Laughter began to buoy me up. What shuts down problem making? Where is this fear coming from, and what are its effects? What is this ambition about? What kind of desire is this? Why am I so obsessed with presenting at this conference?

Finally, I had to go way down into a very painful place, to be lost, before I could begin to discover the joy again. I had to be confronted with my vulnerability, my imperfection, my ego. I nearly drowned in the violence of my own self-absorption, a self-disgust born of the very text of my life, born of the will to power. The self-negation had shut down my ability to think until I was so frustrated that I could not bear it. I had to wait until that moment for something else to kiss me.

Something Else: Love, Truth, the Educated Third

That something else is born of the same text of my life, but it is not about power. I don't really have a name for it. It doesn't really exist as a thing or a body. Perhaps this is what Serres (1997) calls the "educated third." Perhaps we could name it "love"—Or "the good," or "truth." Our words will not capture what it is, and yet it is only because we struggle to name it that it keeps returning. Born of the limit space and the generative force of difference circulating there, it is what makes it possible to struggle for justice in the world. I had to wait for the love of the truth to become stronger than my ego. When that love came, I found the courage to peer over the edge again, to face the limit space—to write, and to think, and to ask my questions. These are the necessary conditions for education, for teaching and learning, and for a more just world.

Those of us in academia know all too well what comes to interfere with the will to truth. We are all too familiar with the will to power and its ugly effects. The institutions that we work in thrive on competition and rivalry. Violence is a part of our daily lives there, producing and reproducing the psychological, social, and even ritual relations that I have been describing. I am not suggesting that we could easily escape their effects.

Nor am I suggesting that we should rid ourselves of the desire for love or affirmation, or even that such a desire necessarily leads to violence. Rather, I am pointing out contradictions that seem to plague us: our need to transcend our imperfection although we will never close the gap between the world and our attempts to represent it or between what we "know" and what we do not. Perhaps that is what needs to be affirmed, this "me" that will never be full, but is always fuller than we imagine.

Instead, we trap ourselves in the belief that we could somehow avoid the problem of imperfection or gain power over it through the fullness of self, of "me." And, in so doing, we stop the necessary ethical struggle, the attention to and compassion for others. And this includes the other "me" that is, in fact, yet to come. In short, we stop educating ourselves and others.

The Question of Gender

When I first wrote and presented this paper, I steered clear of the question of gender that circulates in this story. I'm not sure why, except that I was somehow not ready to confront it. I do think it is an important piece of the dynamic that needs to be addressed if we are to understand what goes on for women and men as we struggle within these academic settings as teachers and as students. I do not pretend to be able to do that in the necessary depth here, but I do want to say something about it and perhaps point to what needs to be done.

Clearly, the desire for truth is shot through with relations of power and identity that include gender. The ability to ask questions in particular contexts and the ability to have them heard is not the same for men and women because of the ways in which we come to be defined and thus think of ourselves as "knowers," or question makers (Taylor, Gilligan & Sullivan, 1995; Bartky, 1996; Luke, 1996; Orenstein, 1994). Did I run to my mother with my questions hoping that she, a woman, would be the one to confirm them? Was my disappointment about some perception that she could not or would not engage me this way? Did she not engage me because of her own self-negation as a knower? Or out of some fear that I might be hurt if I began to understand myself as able to ask questions of the world?

All these questions swirl through this text and I must admit that I cannot clearly answer any of them with any certainty. But I suspect that the dynamics they suggest are relevant, and that the self-violence that I periodically engage is caught in the politics of gender, desire, and identity. What happens if we entertain Girard's theory and invite gender politics to play a part in mimetic desire? Why was my model a man? What dynamics got played out with him that would not have been there if he were a woman? Some of these questions will be addressed in the next chapter as I explore the question of developing femininity and masculinity in the context of schools and peer relations.

Girls—and boys, for that matter—are born into and grow up in a culture in which social relations are hierarchized by gender. Identities are made in participation with a powerful system of meaning that presents men and boys as stronger, smarter, and more apt to achieve independent, autonomous lives simply by virtue of their gender. In a culture structured by male dominance and, moreover, by compulsory heterosexuality, as Adrienne Rich (1983) has taught us, the question of how gender plays in the dynamic of mimetic desire becomes important. To what extent and in what ways is "fullness of being" and the role of model represented as masculine and played out for women by men? I'm certain that in my own life my father was such a figure, and though I have had women who were mentors, none have had the impact on me that male figures have had. Much of the history of feminist research has been focused on the ways that forms of fullness get coded in masculine terms and used as the standard for humanity.

Certainly, the problem of imperfection must be experienced differently, perhaps more violently, by women than it is by men. Women have, after all, been defined historically in Western discourses—medical, philosophical, and popular—as imperfect men. With men's experiences viewed as the standard, these discourses and their accompanying identity formations produce a kind of double jeopardy of imperfection for women. The desire for affirmation and the potential for self-negation in this context seems particularly dangerous.

Looking at my own case, I am not surprised that I did not take the opportunity of success to engage in a rivalry with my mentor. I could not since I did not see myself as even close to his equal. Instead, I engaged the competition with myself and experienced intense self-defeat as I turned the violence inward. It seems to me that this tendency is not uncommon for women, especially given the systematic processes of inferiorization that we experience daily. Moreover, women and girls do not generally grow up learning how to fight, but instead how to be self-sacrificing, passive, and nurturing creatures.[2]

Many women, in fact, learn that the varying degrees of violence they receive daily—psychological, symbolic, and physical—is what they deserve as women. Schools, families, and the media are just some of the more potent sites where such a pedagogy of shame occurs (Bartky, 1996; Bordo, 1996). Self-abdication is just part of the fallout of this cultural dynamic. Listening carefully to Weil, I'm interested in the ways that social and self-violence shut down our ability to engage as thoughtful and thought-provoking participants in the struggles against injustice and toward a better world. What damage must it do to our efforts to engage ethically, politically, and pedagogically in the world? What openings might such suffering provide? These questions will be pursued in the chapters to come.

Obviously, women as well as men continue to be thrilled by the desire for truth and to engage the questions that come. And, in spite of our socialization, women are clearly not immune to the desire for power that lurks in the shadows of this work and the resulting relations we create with others. But though I continue to be critically interested in the specificity of women's lives, these contradictory desires generate problems that also exceed the boundaries of gender.

On Schooling

Is there really an ego? Perhaps it is a conventional way of saying something about this desire for power and all the effects produced as we use language, as we try to say something about or seek a definition of ourselves in this world. I'm not sure I understand desire yet. I do know what disappointment is, however; I've felt it in my gut. And I know the joy that questions can bring; I've felt that down my spine and in my chest, a mixture of pride and surprise. Every teacher knows this feeling. It's what makes teaching worth all the struggle and exhaustion. But schools and classrooms, even college classrooms, are not always places where questions and the desire for truth are nurtured and flourish.

Too many classrooms are places where the teacher is believed to be in the place of fullness or certainty, holding the answers, while the students struggle to prove themselves capable of attaining such heights. Or perhaps worse, students often simply stop caring, sinking into indifference about themselves or the world. Either way, the violence to self and others in these classrooms is too well known. The desire for recognition in this game is framed by hierarchical relations of power structured by the social relations of the school itself, and caught in forms of domination that often lead to jealousy and other dangerous, even violent effects. And, as I have tried to demonstrate in this chapter, too often our desire for power overcomes the will to truth, impeding the generative effects of pedagogy.

To Love the Questions Is to Care for the Truth

To care for the truth is to wait for the questions, and perhaps to give them, but not as a matter of exchange. The care of the truth has nothing to exchange since it is a matter of accepting a moment of emptiness opened by a question, a space that forms the limits on our thought, or a limit that gives form to our thought. This space, too often difficult to accept, is the condition for thinking itself. And also for teaching.

To learn to love the questions is really a matter of learning to learn or, better, learning to feel at ease in the uncertainty, even anxiety, brought on by the spaces opened up when one allows the questions to flutter into the open. Even more, I believe learning to love the questions is a matter of beginning to feel at ease with a certain responsibility opened by the care of the truth. It is a responsibility governed by the necessity to choose, to make a decision, to struggle with the problem of value. And this is where the problem of ethics in education issues forth.

Standing at the edge of the unthought, even the unasked, and always the unsaid, is the moment of choosing. The choice is about what is "good," not as an *a priori* form waiting to be discovered, but rather as something to be decided upon and wrestled with. I mean that it is ultimately this question, what is the best way, that we are confronted with as members of any community. And it is this problem that students and teachers too must learn to love. No matter what we choose, the question of what is the best or right way will always come back, again and again in an infinite repetition. And though we can never finally answer, we must try. That's what it means to care.

To stand on this edge, "to endure it," as Weil says, is an event, the ethical event of the question itself. I also hear Heidegger: "The indefinability of Being does not eliminate the question of its meaning; it demands that we look that question in the face" (1962, p. 23).

If we stand, waiting on this edge, something happens: a question, an idea, or a word that touches, stabs, caresses, burns. Something to propel us toward an answer. If we turn away, we turn away from the care of the world, and ultimately, ironically, tragically from the care of ourselves. To become educated is to attend to a kind of waiting. And this is precisely what it means for teachers and students to learn to love the questions.

To wait for the question is not to remain passive. Quite the contrary. It is to expend as much energy as possible in the attention to a problem. To push for the right word, even as none come, or as too many flood our paper or our discussions with our students. It is to force our way up to the precipice, to that limit space. To wait for the question as that event that will again open us to some possible expressions, some ways to care.

That is the event that we must be worthy of, serene with. To choose and to choose again, even through all our errors, even through our most selfish, or self-effacing moments. To wait for the question is to think; it is not a matter of knowing, or of certainty, or even of comfort. If we believe that a problem is simply a matter of overcoming uncertainty, we will be perpetually trapped in sadness and afflicted by the disappointing sense of failure. This is the ego's territory.

I know I need to say something more about education, perhaps specifically about teaching, but when I sit down to do it, I find that this something more eludes me. I take my dog to the park, and we sit in the grass with the sun on us. I think about Plato's sun and Deleuze's grass, two powerful metaphors for the truth. I think about the differences between these metaphors, their very different effects for thinking about thinking and about teaching. Plato's heights, Deleuze's surface; grass growing in whatever cracks open. That's a little like my sense of the constancy of questions; they spring up because of the cracks, the limit spaces in our words and our thinking (Deleuze & Parnet, 1987).

To teach is to bring our questions to others, to share as teachers and as students in this process of thinking about who we are on this earth. That means facing the paradoxical space that circulates in our attempts to say or write or teach about this life and this Earth, and facing the constant and beautiful return of the question and our imperfection at answering. Therefore, teachers must learn to listen to and engage the questions posed by their students, even and perhaps especially when these questions are suprising or disconcerting, when they do not conform to preconceived expectations and goals. Yes, teachers *with* their students must learn to love the questions. That is the condition of education that we must be at peace with. It is indeed the condition for joy, for loving the world and ourselves as part of it.

To be writing this now is a pragmatics of such a love. We have only our analogies, our stories, our translations of the circumstances of our lives. As Michel Serres so passionately and tenderly writes, "densely sown in the determinate, the possible accompanies us all through time. Without these temporal plateaus mixed with valleys, there would be no hope, no future; there would never be any change (1991, p. 47).

I write this and I teach for the hope brought by the questions that spring from spaces between my writing and the grass, and for those with whom I'd like to share the wonder of green.

Notes

1. I take this phrase and much of my thinking about the "me" from Jacques Derrida: "The ear of the other says me to me and constitutes the autos of my autobiography" (1985b, p. 51).

2. Recent research on adolescent girls bears this out. See, for example, Lyn Michael Brown and Carol Gilligan, *Meeting at the Crossroads: Women's Psychology and Girls' Development* (1992); Mary Bray Pipher, *Reviving Ophelia: Saving the Selves of Adolescent Girls* (1994); and Valerie Walkerdine, *Schoolgirl Fictions* (1990).

Chapter 5

Maybonne and Me

Gender, Desire, and Education
in My Perfect Life

By the time I was in eighth grade, most of the questions that had gurgled and swirled in me as a little girl were safely stored away someplace. I don't remember asking "big" questions about the universe or the world, at least not out loud, until much later.[1] But I did get very good at questioning and analyzing in a most outspoken way all the relationships and goings on in my little world, especially those involving the girls and boys in my school. The questions that I raised and the interpretations that I made about who was doing what with whom in junior high and high school often got me in a lot of trouble with my friends. Looking back, I see that those were some of the most painful years of my life; nevertheless, I developed a sense of myself as having something to say about my world, and saying it. For a girl in eighth grade, that can be dangerous.

In this chapter I explore the relationship between gender and desire, looking specifically at the ways that development of adolescent femininity can form barriers to becoming educated for girls. That is, I am interested in untangling some of the processes that block girls' abilities to engage the generative pedagogical processes that swirl around them critically and ethically. What forces and what desires come to undermine girls' creative powers of thought?

While I am particularly concerned with the ways that girls and women develop forms of feminine desire in relation to violent forms of masculinity, and how these forms get repeated and reproduced in their day-to-day lives, I will also argue that these forms are in no way unified or inevitable. Constantly interacting within a complex generative context, girls are not simply passive recipients of patriarchal or misogynist messages. Like boys, they develop alternative and therefore often contradictory forms of desire (the desire to know, for example), which constantly threaten the dominance of existing patriarchal relations. Important questions, interpretations, and reinterpretations that get raised in a particular context help to form these altered identities. There is always the possibility for different forms (of practice, of relation, of subjectivity) to come into play that will then undermine or shift what has come before.

Sunday Morning

It's Sunday morning, and I've just come home from a leisurely late breakfast with a friend and his 12-year old daughter, Sheila. I'm trying to rev myself up to work. My problematic: The construction of femininity and masculinity as these interfere with becoming educated or, specifically, with the ability to make ethical choices. The topic is daunting, and I'm in a familiar mode of resistance. I sit down at the dining room table to flip through a recent issue of *Rolling Stone* which my friend had recently purchased for his daughter. "It's got to be better than *Seventeen*!" he said to me. On the cover is the newest "hot babe" from Hollywood, 18-year-old Alicia Silverstone, teenage star of the summer's blockbuster movie, *Clueless*. Perched in a tiptoed squat position, wide-eyed and innocent, she is (un)dressed in an undersized pink tee shirt and frilly pink underpants, the kind you see on two-year-old toddlers. Her long blond hair falls over her shoulders and is topped with a pink cowgirl hat. Balancing there on her toes and index fingers, she looks vulnerable and unsteady, anything but strong or even close to adult. I feel my stomach turn. When I look inside I'm even more dismayed. There she is again, still in her toddler underwear, flat on her back, legs splayed, crotch open to the camera, holding a big stuffed pink elephant above her head. Another shot shows her sitting cross-legged, also with her crotch open, hugging the same pink toy, this time with a too-small pink top hat sitting crooked on her head. Is this our teenage girl idol? Is this what Sheila has as her model of femininity? The opening line of the article reads, "Alicia Silverstone is the kittenish 18-year-old movie star whom lots of men want to sleep with." Though that may be true, the article goes on to say that poor beautiful Alicia actually leads a boring life, leaving me wondering exactly what that means. Is the idea here that Alicia's life would be meaningful if she were to accept the sexual attention of lots of men? Poor beautiful Alicia?

I think about this production of the infantilized sex queen, of the time 12-year-old Sheila spends in front of a mirror donning just the right touches of makeup trying to appear older, of her best friend who is very bright and athletic but suddenly began speaking with childish intonations, making silly "I don't have a brain in my head" statements, and moving with a clear lack of coordination as soon as she entered junior high.

Suddenly I'm in eighth grade, standing in front of the mirror, trying on my denim hot pants and light brown sleeveless turtleneck. Mark told me he liked how I looked in those short shorts. I lean into the mirror. Green eye shadow or not? Would my mother notice? How was I going to convince her to allow me to go downtown tonight? Is it really possible that Mark, one of the most popular boys and top hockey players, wants to go out with me and not Victoria? All the girls were there when Beverly told me. My heart was pounding!

Refocusing my attention, Alicia Silverstone's image looms before me again. What are girls (and women) learning about their sexuality through these kinds of representation? What forms of desire and femininity are being created in a culture that still defines feminine value in terms of the ability to become "guy magnets," as announced by *Seventeen Magazine*. On the one hand, we have a 12-year-old trying her best to look 20, and on the other, an 18-year-old posing in sexually explicit positions dressed in infant wear. I open the newspaper and read an editorial on a debacle over the Calvin Klein ad campaign portraying teenage girls in various erotic positions, barely dressed, and even undressing. On the very next page is a full-page ad for The Gap portraying a group of boys and girls, all teens, with one girl in the group in a tight sweater with all the buttons but one undone to expose her bare nubile body beneath. It's not the girl's displayed sexuality that bothers me; it's something about its commodification: sex sells and women's bodies are usually used to do the selling. Last week I had an argument with a male acquaintance who described his new practice of using women employees to lure male customers into business deals ("Hey, the Japanese do it. It's in *Forbes Magazine*! Get the guy a date!"). He went on to bemoan the woman competitor who used her own sexual prowess to beat him out and win a contract that he wanted ("She's a bitch." He might have said "slut.").

What is all this about? These images and stories are part of the complex discursive and economic context within which contemporary adolescent femininity and masculinity (which obviously become adult femininity and masculinity) develop. It is, at a more personal level, the context that I grew up in and now write and teach in. I want to say something about how desire and femininity get represented or constructed for young girls and how such constructions form significant barriers to becoming educated. This is difficult business for me, as I struggle against the flood of memories—many very painful—that come as I think about these issues. I write against the grain of my own life to examine how certain forms of femininity and desire function in girls' and women's lives to prevent the forms of public and personal engagement around ethical and political decision making needed to participate as active, fair, and effective members in their relationships, communities, and the larger world.

The fundamental question is this: If girls are being taught that their value is in their sexualized bodies and not in their abilities to ask and pursue important questions about themselves in the world, how can they possibly engage in the forms of political action and ethical questioning necessary to transform the world? How can their desire for truth be activated within such a context?

In the previous chapter, drawing on René Girard's work, I wrote that desire is culturally learned and maintained through complex sociosymbolic systems in which we live, and that certain forms of desire are at the heart of the perpetuation of social and psychic violence and subjugation. In this chapter, I want to look further at the ways that the social construction of desire—in this case, white heterosexual adolescent masculine and feminine desires and identities—cross paths and are implicated in the maintenance of and resistance to forms of masculine violence and patriarchal power. Drawing on feminist reinterpretations of Foucault's famous dictum that "the individual is an effect of power" (1980, p. 98), I will argue that these forms of feminine and masculine desire, while psychologically structured, are created within existing sociosymbolic relations, practices, and organizations, including schooling, and are at the heart of the failure to develope more ethical ways of living together for both men and women.

In addition, I will argue that "the feminine," while historically constituted in relation to masculine forms that often include domination and even brutality, asserts itself or has the potential to assert itself as something more than a subjugated persona. The feminine is not merely a subjugated form or subject. Contradictory configurations of desire open cracks in subjugated identities, producing the potential for different orientations, decisions, actions, and ways of being (Cornell, 1993; Gutterman, 1994). In this sense, as I have been arguing throughout this book, education defined as the ability to engage an ethical orientation to the world and critical judgments aimed at making one's own and others' lives better becomes possible through openings produced by the generative force of difference. Such possibilities are made in a variety of social-relational or pedagogical contexts.

This chapter analyzes again the ways in which desires conflict, the ways in which an ethical and political problematizing persona inserts itself into and disrupts subjugating forms of desire. Here I'm talking about the ways that desire for transformation intersects and shifts or challenges dominating gender relations, even if only momentarily, leading to passages toward different ways of living and being. So while I'm interested in what comes to block the development of educated/ethical subjects, I also want to explore how contradictory desires can coexist and even struggle together to produce openings toward becoming educated.

I will explore these complex issues by weaving moments in my own life with an analysis of the life of a fictional girl, Maybonne Mullen, the heroine of cartoonist Lynda Barry's well-known strip, "Ernie Pook's Comeek." I fell in love with this comic strip and especially with the story of Maybonne and her little sister Marlys several years ago. Their story pulsates with the questions of the relation between desire, identity, and education, making Lynda Barry an important contemporary cultural critic. Barry's work sheds light on the contextualized forces, codes, and representations that contribute to the constitution of feminine desires and identities through her portrayal of Maybonne as she makes her way through the world of school and friendship.

We see up close the struggles of a young girl around all these issues, and we are forced to remember ourselves in those struggles, our implication in the relations creating specific social forms and our ethical responsibility for challenging those forms in whatever ways that we can.

An Introduction to My Perfect Life

I walk into class. The room is buzzing with the usual conversations that precede our more formal discussion of the week's reading. This is the graduate seminar on Popular Culture and Education that I teach. This week's topic is gender and the politics of identity. There are eight or nine women and only two men. They were assigned Lynda Barry's My Perfect Life *(1992). "So, what did you think? How did you find Maybonne's story?" The room erupts into a chorus of women's voices. "Oh my God! I'm Maybonne!" "This is* my *story." The men sit silently.*

Lynda Barry's comic book, *My Perfect Life*, chronicles a year in the life of an all too typical teenage girl, Maybonne Mullen. Maybonne is white and lives with her grandmother and her little sister. Perhaps not so typical, their mother lives "halfway across the country" (they're not sure where their father is). She left them with their grandmother last year while they were supposedly visiting on vacation. Living with Grandma isn't bad, but it's no picnic. And as we find out, being a new girl in school has not been easy for Maybonne either. From what we can tell in the story, her school or at least her peer group is homogeneously white. Told through Maybonne's letters to her friend Brenda, to herself, and to God, the comic strip chronicles with painful accuracy a young girl's experiences of and reflections upon school, sexuality, love, friendship, and family life. Maybonne's writings function for Barry as an analysis of the complex politics of desire and identity as they are constructed within the relations of day-to-day school and family life.

I have used this book several times with students in a graduate seminar on Popular Culture and the Politics of Education and have heard the same responses from my women students each time. "This is a book about me! Oh my God! I'm Maybonne." Meanwhile the few male students in my classes have generally responded either that they can't relate or that they recognize this story as someone else's experience, not theirs.

These responses don't surprise me since this is a story primarily about the play of desire in the constitution of female identity. I too recognize myself in Maybonne. Indeed, so strong has been my identification with her story that I used to run to the corner pub each Thursday where I'd pick up my free copy of the *Metro Times*, turn to the back, and read the latest installment in Maybonne's saga. Learning that these strips had been put together in a book, I began to use *My Perfect Life* with students. Oh, the memories that surface and the stories that have been shared in response to this book!

I am compelled to get to the bottom of Maybonne's pain, to unravel the threads that tie my story to hers. I begin this analysis from the conviction that I recognize myself in her, in fact that Barry is able to create this book, because it is a story made within very specific cultural conditions, shared conditions through which specific forms of desire, identity, and hence social relations are made. I understand Maybonne because I am tied to her through the same relational forces that produce me as desiring, thinking, writing, and teaching subject. Perhaps especially for white women (since all her characters are white), this is a book that helps us to "*un*forget" how we have come to be who we are, to look at the processes that have shaped us straight on and to confront ourselves there. As American feminist and cultural critic Drucilla Cornell puts it,

> The condition in which the suffering of all women can be "seen" and "heard" in all of our difference, is that in which the tyranny of established reality is disrupted and the possibility of further feminine resistance and the writing of a different story is affirmed. . . . Woman and women cannot be separated from the fictions and metaphors in which she and they are presented, and through which we portray ourselves. (1993, pp. 2–3)

As a form of feminist writing, Barry's work is just such an exposure and disruption. She both exposes some of the ways that white adolescent feminine desire and sexuality are constituted within a heterosexist framework of male dominance and even brutality, and she offers important insight into how these forms might be disrupted.

We catch up to Maybonne on the first day of school, where we are introduced to her teachers as "a cruddy deal" her lunch time as "scrubbly," and Corinna Morton, a new girl with "a slightly Hee-Haw accent," as a less than desirable locker partner. "I am trying not to be shallow about her defects," Maybonne writes, "because I know the experience of being hard up for friends from last year when I first came here, but I'm trying to find someone to trade partners with. So far no one will. Sometimes I wonder: Is there a curse on my life?" (Barry, 1992, p. 7). Maybonne elaborates on the subject of her teachers with some very funny descriptions: "First Period: Miss Fortner. History. Looks like she has a eternal headache. Has on a ugly wig. . . . Third Period: Mr. Sargus. Music. Spits when he talks and underarm odor and alcohol odor" (p. 6). She also critiques the pedagogy and curriculum she experiences: "He keeps talking about freedom but he doesn't mean the same kind I am into. In his life it's the freedom to boss people and the freedom to make you shut up if you give your argument to his opinion"(p. 9), In all of this, we are immediately confronted with a tension in Maybonne's life between her own critical consciousness and desire to think and speak for herself and a primary problematic of acceptance and affirmation as it frames the lives of girls in schools, namely, the people one associates with can mean the difference between being in or out, and whether one is in or out of the group can mean the difference between happiness and hell.

"True Experience"

I'm walking down the hall with a girlfriend. "Gross! Did you see what Shelly wore to gym class! She probably bought those shorts in Newberry's! And her shirt had holes in it," Frances was laughing. "Shelly's poor; I don't think you should laugh," I say back, but she's already onto something else. "Hey, did you see cheerleading practice yesterday?" "Yeah," I say, "I think the whole thing is stupid and I can't see why they want to be cheerleaders, but I really think Beverley's the only one who's any good. I wouldn't pick any of the rest." That afternoon a note goes around saying Shelly's my best friend and that I said I don't like any of the girls in my gang. No one would sit with me or talk to me for two weeks.

As noted in many studies of adolescent girls, association has value and defines who one is (Brown & Gilligan, 1992; Orenstein, 1994; Pipher, 1994; Taylor, Gilligan, & Sullivan, 1995; Tanenbaum, 1999). The power of association and group affirmation becomes very clear when Maybonne is unexpectedly cast out of her group of friends. When one of her girlfriends, Nancy Newby, tells her a story of the appearance of "a ghostly hand" one night when she went into the bathroom to pee, Maybonne is convinced it's true because "no one would logically make up a story with yourself peeing in it" (Barry, 1992, p. 13). Determined to get to the bottom of the mystery and help her friend, she decides that they should do a seance in the bathroom of the school in order to draw the hand away from Nancy's bathroom. They are caught holding hands in a toilet stall. Suddenly, Maybonne's gesture to help her friend

Lynda Barry, *My Perfect Life*, p. 12

and thus be affirmed as loyal is turned upside down. Now the rumors fly around the school via her ex-girlfriends that she and Nancy Newby are "lesbian queers together" (p. 16).

Eventually singled out for her known refusal to join in her friends' homophobia, Maybonne is shunned:

> I said this thing one time about what's wrong with queers? Because Sue Acker (the bitch!) (I'm going to write bitch every time after her name because she is a bitch. A bitch to the 10th power!) Because she is always saying everyone's a queer. . . . Her whole life is who's a queer and how I'm a queer because I don't think queers are weird, but I was even stupid to say it because I forgot this is a plastic world so if you have a free mind, better shut up . . . (p. 17)

In the cartoon underneath this narrative, presumably written in a letter to her friend Brenda, we see Maybonne desperately trying to catch up with Nancy to walk home after school. Nancy takes off, leaving Maybonne standing alone. She discovers "lesbo" written on her locker and her friends refuse to eat lunch with her.

Barry exposes in the behaviors of these fictional girls the complex politics of association and rivalry in a context structured by compulsory heterosexuality and sexual competition. As girls round the corner of adolescence and stumble onto the sexual marketplace, they find themselves in a confusing, competitive milieu where the stakes are high but the rules are not always clear. Desire, rivalry, and a certain meanness circulate in school hallways and cafeterias as girls strive to maintain association and constitute their identities within the right group, that is, the group that will produce the most value in the competition for prized male attention.

As Maybonne finds out, this association and the affirmation that accompanies it are fragile, easily exploded by the most innocent of gestures. Laws governing acceptance and affirmation and thus motivating desire derive from the needs and demands of patriarchy that produces for girls (and women) a context of competition for male attention, affirmation, and even possession. All this occurs within an institutional context which is structured by hierarchical, bureaucratized patriarchal relations and explicit expectations for compulsory heterosexuality.

Introducing gender politics into the work of René Girard, we can see a kind of reciprocal violence unfolding, precipitated through the verbal exchange of girls. This is a violence made of the desire for value within a group defined through their success at achieving "normal" femininity, or what Maybonne terms "being real." Maybonne is pushed out of the group through the practice of homophobia in order that the other girls may more definitively identify with "normal" femininity. Kicking someone out of the group as she threatens this value or critiques some part of the dynamics therein is a move made to keep a kind of stability and unity and generate power among the members. As I will develop, the violence that the girls engage with each other around association is directly related to socially structured and learned male dominance and the attending desire for heterosexual possession and exploitation of the available girls.

In this sense, at least part of what Maybonne experiences in the homophobia of her friends is a practice of scapegoating that helps to define the dominance of heterosexual relations and keeps the rivalry within the group under control. Early in the story Maybonne identifies herself as having a radical perspective on the question of homosexuality (as well as on the concept of freedom more generally), and she pays for such an identification via peer group politics. By scapegoating Maybonne, the other girls unify themselves around a feminine norm accepting the demands of compulsory heterosexuality and thus solidifying the requisite definitions of femininity and masculinity. As the story continues, we see just how powerful these demands are in the social construction of desire.

"What Is Better?"

Maybonne is in a pickle. She has been cast out of her group for expressing her belief that "queers are equal to anybody" and accused of being a lesbian. "No girls will talk to me and boys shout lesbo," but shortly a solution presents itself. A boy named Doug asks her if she would like to prove that

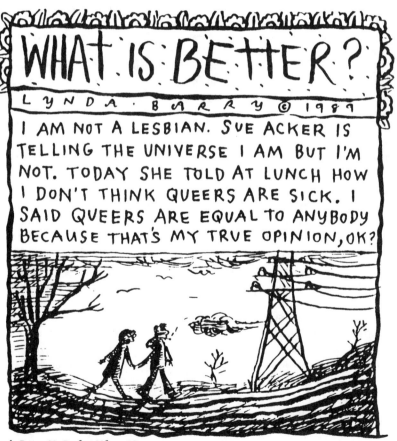

Lynda Barry, *My Perfect Life*, p. 18

she is not a lesbian, mentioning "things about balling." Maybonne allows him to put his arm around her so that Sue Acker sees. "Is it better to be a lesbian or a slut?" With this question hovering in all its complex significance, she goes with him after school to a place near his house and allows him to touch her breasts. "Tomorrow he'll tell them and I promise I'll shut up about queers. I promise" (Barry, 1992, pp. 18–19).

This is very risky business for Maybonne. In order to get back into the group she does the thing that all girls understand to be a death knell in the game of association and feminine value. She risks being identified as a slut.

Leora Tanenbaum has presented in very poignant terms the process of denigration and ostracizing that girls labeled as "sluts" go through and the complex, often contradictory context that produces it.

> Slut-bashing as I call it is one issue that affects every single female who grows up in this country because any preteen or teenage girl can become a target. "Slut" is a pervasive insult applied to a broad spectrum of American adolescent girls, from the girl who brags about one night stands to the girl who has never even kissed a boy to the girl who has been raped. . . . Some girls are called "sluts" because other girls dislike or envy them, and spread a sexual rumor as a form of revenge. Very often the label is a stand in for something else: the extent to which a girl fails to conform to the idea of normal appearance and behavior. (1999, p. 11)

Maybonne is at risk of becoming a target of slut-bashing on many counts— her relatively "new girl" status, her outspoken radical opinions on issues like homosexuality, and now her need to be defined as "normal." She denies that she is homosexual, and yet she openly criticizes her "friends" for their homophobia. She turns to Doug to prove her heterosexual correctness. In her story, we see the weaving together of the problem of slut-bashing within the competitive context of adolescent sexuality and association. By going off with Doug and hoping that he'll set the record straight, Maybonne sets off a series of experiences and events that accelerate the dynamics of rivalry and mimetic desire in the girls' group, as well as a repetitious series of longing and exploitative sexual activity that forms part of the requirements of Doug's developing masculinity.

Looking at the first series, Girard's theory is useful. He argues that desire is produced in a mimetic structure where we desire what we believe to be the object of our model's desire, and this creates a violent rivalry within groups. Thus, the other's value and function as model hinges on the value of the desired object. Believing ourselves to be "empty" as long as we do not possess what the other has, we strive to possess that object in order to be full, or to get the power we believe will fulfill us.

The model for Maybonne is really plural, the other girls in her class who seem to Maybonne to have it together, "to be for real and free." What they have is a position in the group and thus the potential to have the legitimate desire and attention of boys. "Most of all I just wish for everything about me to change. And then I swear to God I would quit acting insecure, and *Be Myself*, like in all the songs where people are being themselves. I would stop faking and be for real and act free like Sue Acker and them" (Barry, 1992, p. 91). Maybonne wants desperately to "have it together, to be real" and especially not to be excluded from the group of girls that form her community and peer group. Wanting to fit into "normal" feminine definitions and thus "be for real," which is especially defined through the dominance of heterosexuality, Maybonne puts her reputation on the line. As Tanenbaum makes clear, "a girl's sexual status is a metaphor for how well she fits into the American ideal of femininity" (1999, p. 3).

The desired object is Doug and here one particular girl in the group, Cindy Ludermyer, becomes an important figure for Maybonne. We find out that she too is seeing Doug, and moreover, she is a leader in the group of girls. A serious rivalry begins between Maybonne and Cindy Ludermyer, escalating the conflict between Maybonne and the group. As Girard points out

> Rivalry does not arise because of the fortuitous convergence of two desires on a single object; rather, the subject desires the object because the rival desires it. In desiring an object the rival alerts the subject to the desirability of the object. The rival then, serves as a model for the subject, not only in regard to such secondary matters as style and opinions, but also and more essentially, in regard to desires. (1977, p. 145)

This raises an interesting twist for Maybonne and for girls and women more generally I think, ultimately leading into the second series of exploitive relations with Doug, the object of this rivalrous dynamic.

"The Suddenly Magical"

Maybonne's first desire is acceptance and affirmation by her female peers, which she seeks by confirming her love object to be a man. The girls are her models, he is only the tool through which she can become fully acceptable. But, to really fit in, to get the *affirmation* and value she seeks, she has to get the sexual game right, to prove herself capable and desirable while remaining a good girl. She has to prove to herself and to her friends that Doug loves her. If she fails, she's just a slut.

My brother is taunting me. "I heard you slept with him." I'm running up the stairs toward my bedroom. "Shut up!" "Slut!" he calls after me. I whirl around, screaming, "Mike loves me!" He just laughs.

THE "SUDDENLY MAGICAL" ISN'T GOING TO HAPPEN TO ME. EXCEPT ONE WAY ONLY: IF DOUG WILL BE IN LOVE WITH ME. IF DOUG FEELS ME UP BUT IS IN LOVE, I DON'T COUNT AS A SLUT. WHAT A PERFECT ENDING. IF ONLY I CAN MAKE HIM LOVE ME. IF ONLY I CAN BE JUST PERFECT FOR HIM IT WOULD BE SUCH A BEAUTIFUL ENDING.

WHAT?!

NOTHING.

WANNA GO FOR ANOTHER WALK AGAIN?

Lynda Barry, *My Perfect Life*, p. 21

In the context of rivalry and desire for acceptance, the only way for Maybonne's sexual experiences with Doug to be legitimate is for him to love her. Thus, as her desire for "beautiful love" with Doug grows, she becomes emotionally attached to him. Rather than giving her love and affirmation, however, he turns away and refuses to acknowledge her. He tells his friends that he and Maybonne "balled," a rumor that Maybonne tries to deny by "laughing in their faces." While Doug shows little interest in Maybonne after their initial encounter, Maybonne is, of course, convinced that he is perfect for her. She writes him a letter:

Dear Doug,

You know that song by Sly and the Family Stone, "Everybody is a Star"? the words go: *Everybody is a star I can feel it when you shine on me.* There's people at this school who say you are the kind that uses girls. But when I hear that song I only think of you. For one thing the song is beautiful and I think you are a beautiful person. . . . Some girls whose names I won't tell tried to bring me down at lunch by saying you said some things about me like how flat I am. Also that we balled. I just laughed in their faces and then I kept on truckin' because from knowing you like I do it's so obviously a lie that you would ever say anything like that. Another part of the song goes: I love you for who you are not the one you feel you need to be. I hope that doesn't make you feel weird but it's true. . . . (Barry, 1992, p. 22)

At the bottom of the narrative we see a boy teasing Doug as he reads the letter. "'I think you are a beautiful person' . . . hey, man you said you did it with her . . . she says you're lyin" (pp. 22–23).

Governing the situation are the rules and processes of association and affirmation as it functions for boys in the construction of a dominating heterosexual masculinity. For Doug, masculine value is gauged according to sexual prowess and exploitation, and as the story continues, we see a repetitious series of approach, attention, and withdrawal that plays on Maybonne's need to define him as a beautiful person who is perfect for her. "Oh Doug the tragedy of life is how perfect you are for me. I always knew it before, but when you quit liking me I knew it for sure" (p. 25).

Indeed, he is "perfect" as the object that will prove her heterosexuality, as well as heighten her status as a rival, and construct for her, once again, the absence and sense of lack needed to fuel these dynamics. Girard's analysis of the vertigo that plays in such violent structures of desire is important. Maybonne moves from being in love, to recognizing and experiencing shame at Doug's exploitive behavior, to moving out of her "lovesick" state, only to have the process begin again.

I walk into the Side Track, the corner pub. There's my friend Wendy. I met her a year or so ago when she took my Pop Culture course. "Hey! How's it going?" She gives me a hug. We chat. Eventually she says, "So are you still broken up with Tom?" I look at my shoes. "I knew it! Rebecca, he's your Doug!"

After 27 days, just when she is feeling better, Doug reappears, and life becomes "magical" once again. But the magical heavenly moment becomes hell all too quickly as Maybonne realizes that Doug is seeing Cindy publicly while telling her that their love must remain a secret. This time she writes to God:

> Dear God, No offense but I am wondering about you. . . . I mean thank you and all [for sending Doug back] but this thing where he says I can't tell anybody that he's my boyfriend, I think sort of sucks. . . . Remember I asked for beautiful love with him. If this is beautiful please show me how. I need some hints bad. . . . My question is what are you going to do if Cindy Ludermyer prays for Doug also? Is she more equal than me? . . . My life feels so messed up. In the name of the father, the son, and the holy ghost if it turns out Doug is just using me I will die. (pp. 34–35)

More than anything Maybonne wants to believe the relationship is "true and beautiful," even while she "knows" that he is lying and "doing her cold-blooded" by seeing Cindy. In order to remain attached (and stay popular with and affirmed by her peers), she has to construct Doug's motivations as beautiful and "true," (otherwise she'll have to succumb to the identity of slut) even while she "knows" otherwise. She dissociates from what she knows to be true in order to negotiate the forces that are in play. To value herself, Maybonne has to maintain an identity as a good girl: desirable, loving, and lovable. Sex in any other relationship is "slutty" and results in soiled femininity. So she reaches out to Doug and tells him she knows that inside he's really beautiful and good, defining him as such in order to convince herself of her own goodness (read "normal" unsoiled femininity).

As Nancy Chodorow (1978), Carol Gilligan (1982), and others have shown us, for girls, identification with their mothers as ethical caregivers governs their developing femininity. And as Jessica Benjamin (1988) and John Brenkman (1993) make clear, this gendered psychological development must be understood within the sociosymbolic context of male-dominated compulsory heterosexuality. Maybonne tries to be a caretaker of Doug's goodness, certain that he could not really want to be who he thinks he must, that is, who he must within the misogynist demands of masculine culture. She has to dissociate from the process he is in, in order to show him how much she cares for the good person she is sure he is, and thus prove "how perfect for him she is." If only he would love her, then she wouldn't be a slut. The mother/whore dichotomy is in full bloom psychologically and socially, both in Maybonne's struggle for love and acceptance, as well as Doug's construction of himself as a man.

"The Concept of Doug"

As we see in Maybonne's story, girls' identities are wrought within a struggle around double standards of sexual conduct in a context saturated with the mother/whore representation. Exploring insights within psychoanalytic theory, however, we see that this psychosocial representation is kept firmly

Lynda Barry, *My Perfect Life*, p. 36

in place by the development of heterosexual masculinity. Complicated and common, the mother/whore dichotomy has been a lynchpin of the Oedipus complex laid out by Freud and, later, Lacan who argue that it is a result of a "universal tendency to debasement in male heterosexual development."

For Freud and Lacan, the debasement of women is the result of a failure in the adolescent boy's psyche of two currents: sensuality and affection. Here debasement "refers to the moral, aesthetic, and social valuation by means of which the man deems a woman his inferior and on this basis finds her desirable" (Brenkman, 1993, p. 168). The two currents whose union is necessary to ensure a completely normal attitude in love fail to combine leaving the boy and later the man unable to share sexual pleasure with a woman he deems too closely resembling his mother.

In normal development, before and then again during adolescence, these two currents become entwined, and a sensual pleasure becomes combined with affection in the attachment to the mother as love object. Normally, according to Freud, the incest taboo is strong enough to turn the boy's erotic desires away from his mother. When the sexual aim is redirected outside the family (that is, away from the mother as incestuous love object), "the affection and esteem the boy formerly reserved for his mother and sisters will follow along. By the same token, this is the critical point at which the two currents (sensuality and affection) are vulnerable anew to splitting" (Freud, quoted in Brenkman, 1993, p. 167).

In one form of pathological development (development that Freud admits is more the norm than the norm!), the individual's erotic capacities become inhibited and the boy is able to love a woman only so long as his sensual desires are not implicated as well. Esteem and affection become incompatible with pleasure which is only experienced in relation to a debased woman. Thus, according to Freud, the representation of woman as mother/whore is the result of this pathological psychic development of male heterosexual desire. More often than not, it seems, boys' capacities for sexual exploitation, that is, sensual pleasure without the capacity for affection, reign.

Nancy Chodorow's reinterpretation of the Oedipus complex confirms the denigration of women as part of men's normal developmental need to renounce the identification with the mother. A boy represses "those qualities he takes to be feminine within himself, and rejects and devalues women and whatever he considers to be feminine in the social world" (1978, p. 181). Michael Kimmel and Michael Kaufman call this flight from femininity "the mother wound," arguing with Chodorow that, as he recognizes the mother's feminine weaknesses and the need to separate to become a man, "the boy internalizes the categories of gender power of a patriarchal society. The social project is internalized and unconsciously recreated in the psychic life of the young boy" (1994, p. 271).

John Brenkman critiques the universalizing biological model of desire within these psychoanalytic models arguing that

> the forces shaping a son's Oedipal relation to his mother are not any universal or archaic condition of the mother-child relation, but rather the cultural codes and representations which derive from the historical and collective relations between men and women. The psycho-genesis that Freud sought to explain the pathological and the normal tendencies of male [and female] heterosexuality has to be reframed in terms of social genesis and cultural genealogy of the pathologies and norms themselves. (1993, p. 165)

Brenkman argues that it makes more sense to see the ways in which the representation of woman in dichotomous terms as mother/whore actually precedes and constructs the split between affection and sexual desire in boys. While remaining supportive of and revising many of the insights within psychoanalysis, Brenkman echoes Adrienne Rich (1983), arguing for understanding that the context of power within which this gendered representation plays has a long and fertile history, and is thus deeply imbedded in the institutions, day-to-day practices, legal policies, and thus the individual psyches that collectively make up this culture.[2] Individual identity and desire must be analyzed within a complex psychological and cultural process which is structured by specific political and social relations.

The image, as well as the actual subjective position, of girls and women as sluts or good girls is produced and reproduced within the real discursive and sexual relations between boys and girls, especially during adolescence. Schools are primary sites for these complex dynamics to play themselves out. Slut-bashing is an important ritual for both boys and girls within the social-relational and institutional dynamics that form gendered identities, and is generally (tragically) ignored or written off by most school personnel as part of the culture of adolescence, just "what kids do." Clearly, though boys and girls learn their lessons well in this context, as Tanenbaum makes clear, schools are not the only institutions where "boys will be boys" since we see the manifestations of this representation throughout the culture. Women who try to bring sexual harassment complaints are often villainized by coworkers and their institutions as being too sexual, and rape victims often do not bring their cases to court for fear of being further degraded through well-known accusations of "asking for it" (Tanenbaum, 1999).

Barry does not focus on what is going on for Doug when he is not with Maybonne, so we have just a slice of his life to look at here, the slice that touches Maybonne and that she interprets. Admittedly, this leaves us with only those interactions that involve Maybonne and these are always told through Maybonne's eyes. Still, drawing from these interactions and applying Girard's theory here, we might ask who Doug's object of desire is and who his models are? The construction of masculinity is also mimetic to the extent that men seek to be affirmed in the existing cultural and historical representations and relations of domination and compulsory heterosexuality. Because of the existence of patriarchal and misogynist social relations, the same terms of affirmation do not apply for Doug and Maybonne.

Affirmation is clearly what Doug wants, but it is affirmation from his peers around his performance in the game of sexual prowess, conquest, and domination in the making of a certain hegemonic masculinity. Love from Maybonne is simply part of the game to the extent that it keeps her in a kind of submissive vertigo (which, of course, plays off the rivalry already in place in her peer group). For Doug, sexual conquest as a demonstration of power, or at least the appearance of it, depends on her feminine formations of care and acquiescence to assert itself, and thus his actions in pursuit of sexual domination set up the production of psychic violence. In an early assertion of the social construction of masculinity in school contexts, Madeleine Arnot argues that in "a male dominated society femininity is ascribed; in contrast masculinity and manhood have to be 'achieved in a permanent process of struggle and confirmation" (quoted in Mac an Ghaill, 1994, p. 90).

Máirtín Mac an Ghaill develops this in a discussion of findings in his study of masculinity and schooling:

> students are active makers of sex/gender identities, in which they have complex social and psychic investments. . . . Much of this work takes place at a collective level within the informal world of male peer groups, where specific subject positions are inhabited. . . . The persuasiveness to act like heterosexual men circumscribed the peer groups' everyday cultural practices. Sexual orientation was seen as a primary source of identity and social behavior. (1994, p. 91)

Doug's pursuit of Maybonne, his challenge to her that she prove she's not a "lesbo," and his lies to his male friends that he "did it" with her fit this set of demands creating masculine identities in the school setting. Mac an Ghaill, drawing on the empirical evidence in his study as well as the work of other cultural theorists of education (Connell, 1992; Walkerdine, 1992; Weeks, 1989), identifies misogyny, homophobia, and compulsory heterosexuality as the constitutive elements producing differentiated gender identities in schools.

Clearly, it is not just men for whom the heterosexual orientation is important. Girls also perform intense and often hurtful rituals of association and exclusion based upon the demands of male-dominated compulsory heterosexuality. Yet, it is within the male peer groups, as Mac an Ghaill, and others (Connell, 1992; Kaufman, 1993; Weis, 1995) argue, that the standards for compulsory heterosexuality is set and the attending misogynist violence is performed. As Michael Kaufman points out,

> Psychological and sometime physical violence is etched into the body politic of our world through widespread acceptance of discrimination and oppression that casts certain humans as acceptable targets for the wrath of others. . . . In any act of violence, whether sexual harassment, whether a school-yard tussle, a violent display of temper or vicious assault, individual men are acting out relations of sexual and social power. . . .
>
> The starting point is not violence, nor even aggression. It is the boy's unknowing acceptance of the dominant creed of manhood: to be a man we need to shape a personality that can always control and dominate our social and natural environment. . . . The ability to dominate—perhaps only through words or self-control, perhaps through actions—becomes a core feature of masculinity. (1993, pp. 162–163)

Yet, many theorists of masculinity also discuss the contradictory and fragile nature of these seeming monolithic masculine forms. Peer group pressures, emotional ambiguities, contradictory definitions of their female peers, and fears about their own abilities to perform within the demands of patriarchy are reported as evidence of a nexus of subjectivities within shifting relations of power and psychosocial development (Connell, 1992; Kaufman, 1993; Mac an Ghaill, 1994). As Mac an Ghaill reports,

> One of the main difficulties in the research was working through a central dichotomy in many of the young men's lives, namely, their projection of a public confident masculinity and their reporting to me their private anxieties and insecurities. Of particular significance here was their learning the masculine code of splitting sexual practices from emotional feelings. (1994, p. 99)

According to Kaufman (1993), boys and men learn to put up heavy armor against any behavior or emotional experience resembling feminine forms, thus protecting themselves against being viewed as weak or "wussy." Given the misogynist and homophobic atmosphere of the culture generally, it simply is not safe to express any of the "soft" feelings or emotions associated with women or gay men. Boys and men thus often internalize tremendous fear, pain, and confusion, which unfortunately may come boiling out in the only legitimate emotional expression men have access to: anger and an attending violence often activated upon the bodies and psyches of women. And, even when the expression is not particularly violent, it may manifest in a confusing process of attraction and withdrawal from the women and girls in their lives. Connell adds:

> Given the complexity of gender relations no simple or uniform strategy is possible: a "mix" is necessary. So hegemonic masculinity can contain at the same time, quite consistently, openings toward domesticity and openings towards violence, toward misogyny and toward heterosexual attraction. (1987, pp. 185–186)

In *My Perfect Life*, Maybonne finally understands this confusing mix as "the concept of Doug," which she tries to explain to Cindy Ludermyer.

> I know her feeling of loving Doug. When I first went into the girl's can and saw her so messed up, I about did a barf right there on the floor from my relating. It was like smelling the smell of a food you threw up on. I used to have it about Hormel Beef Stew. Now I have it about Doug." (Barry, 1992, p. 37)

Unfortunately for Maybonne, Cindy is still in the throws of her own flood of pain and confusion at Doug's apparent withdrawal of love; she can only hear Maybonne as her rival in the competition for his attention. "I guess love is a deal where you have to learn your own evidence because when I told her someday you will be free she just turned and gave me the deluxe finger" (p. 37).

One of the most interesting parts of this story for me, is Maybonne's ability to critically analyze and even attempt to share what she understands with her rival—to care for her. Circulating within the struggle and rivalry is an ethical capacity that is developed for Maybonne as she writes about her life. Questions surface that disrupt the sadness, and sometimes even turn her suffering into compassion. While I will develop this more fully in the next chapter, I simply want to point to its importance here in offering a potential for something different to emerge in the social relations of this story.

"Marlys Spring"

Just as boys' subjective lives are anything but unified around domination, girls' lives should not be read reductively in terms of simple reactions to masculinity. Even given the dissociated and often rivalrous nature of girls' relationships with each other, the identities that get made are often contradictory and far from simply subjugated in relation to boys. While it often results in hurtful effects, this dynamic relationship among girls also includes the articulation of compassion, loyalty, care, and even activism that is central to the unity of the group and to the strength of girls' ethical development.

Quite apart and different from boys' relationships to each other, girls learn practices of honesty and care that, while often fraught with the very political rivalries that cause conflict, also deepen their capacities for commitment and compassion necessary to opening onto the larger world and ultimately to becoming educated in the sense that I have been defining it in this book. We see this articulation among Maybonne and her girl friends as well as with her little sister, Marlys.

After a series of events surrounding a trip to see her mother over Christmas, involving a run-in with the police who catch her with a boy in the back seat of a car, Maybonne gets very depressed and contemplates killing herself. She asks Cindy Ludermyer if she ever wanted to commit suicide. Cindy says the only reason she didn't is because her "mother would kill her." Writing in her journal about this one night with Marlys asleep beside her, Maybonne thinks about how difficult it would be for Marlys to see her dead: "She has Dad nightmares and Mom nightmares. I don't want to add sister ones"(Barry, 1992, p. 75). Finally, she decides not to kill herself because, as she puts it, "at the last minute I was thinking how I know it would be great to have all my problems gone but how could I even notice it if I was dead?" (p. 76). In the morning Marlys tells her a joke, and Maybonne realizes that if she were dead

Lynda Barry, *My Perfect Life*, p. 82

she'd never see her sister again, or hear that joke, "or see Marlys dancing to the song Soul Finger that's coming out of the radio" (p. 76). She can't stand the idea that she might have caused Marlys, a source of great joy, suffering.

Love for her little sister, as well as the flash of recognition that there could be a different future with her, rescues Maybonne from her self-absorbed sadness, and suddenly she notices the sun shining all over the place. Maybonne's awakening takes her to the bedside of Cindy's father who has just had a stroke. She brings Mr. Ludermeyer a copy of the *Guinness Book of World Records*, her favorite book, sharing with him a story of the oldest known sheep dog. The two of them cry together imagining how bad the owner of that dog must have felt when he died. "Dear Bluey," she writes, "hello from me and Mr. Ludermyer wherever you are" (p. 81).

Soon spring arrives, Marlys dances on the roof singing "Jeremiah was a Bullfrog," much to her grandmother's dismay and Maybonne's delight ("I never knew I loved her so much"), and Maybonne becomes attracted to a new boy, David, leaving behind the competition with Cindy for Doug, at least for the moment. Now she worries that she's too experienced and that David will find out that she "has desires." Mother/whore is always threatening to bring down the "suddenly magical."

"The Truth Session"

Maybonne writes a letter about her worries to Dear Abby, signed "Messed Up and Confused." Then, sharing her thoughts with Sue Acker, Maybonne learns that she has "an inferiority complex," and that the best cure to being a "plastic wall of illusion" is to do "a truth session" with her friends.

I'm in 10th-grade math class. Frieda has intercepted a note to Beverley where I wrote that she should not listen to what the other girls are saying about her relationship with Paul; it's none of their business. Frieda calls a meeting in the girls' locker room after school. They have some things to say to me and I better be there. I go. In one of the larger shower stalls that doesn't work, I am surrounded by about 15 girls. They spend an hour telling me what they think of me. I'm secretly terrified, sweating. One girl, Kelly, tells me that since she moved here last year I have not tried hard enough to be friends with her. "I'm sorry," I say, "I guess I just thought you acted kind of silly all the time." Should I be honest? Another says that she knows I think I'm better than them because I am dating the captain of the hockey team. I feel tiny, about to suffocate. I want them to think I feel perfectly strong. I stand there, mouth dry, trying to swallow. My best friends—Beverly included—are present, but silent. "Keep your chin up" says my mother in my head. I straighten my back for another complaint.

A truth session is sort of group therapy in reverse. The rules are that, instead of listening to Maybonne, the other girls do all the talking, giving their advice and opinions of Maybonne and her personality. Sue tells her it really worked for her cousin from Idaho (Barry, 1992, p. 91). Maybonne wants more than anything to stop feeling terrible (which she says got worse when she found out she has an inferiority complex); she wants the words that come out of her mouth to stop being boring, and she wants just to be beautiful, "like the other girls."

During the session, Cindy Ludermyer accuses Maybonne of "playing herself for cheap" by allowing herself to be used by Doug. Not surprisingly,

Lynda Barry, *My Perfect Life*, p. 89

Maybonne breaks the rules of the session by blurting out that Cindy is "the exact same" as her and she knows it. Cindy starts to cry and suddenly the session turns into a collective expression of compassion for both girls. Maybonne and Cindy walk home together, Cindy apologizes, confessing to her how horrible she had been to Maybonne, and they end up becoming friends. "I didn't even know she was being mean! I just thought that was her natural personality! . . . and now I guess we're friends. Or something" (p. 93).

Or something. First, the truth session functions on one level as a collective expression of policing one of its members: "Here are the problems we see with you. This is what you have to do to change." But when Maybonne interrupts that function with her own interpretation, the girls in the group suddenly turn quite supportive of her. She is granted a degree of power by leader Cindy's gesture of friendship, an action that affirms Maybonne's identity as a critical voice in the group, the very voice that she had been kicked out for using months earlier.

Next, Maybonne is faced with her own survival in a situation she rightly reads as risky. What is interesting here is the simultaneous play of self-protection, compassion, and critical self-reflection. Although there has been a shift in her relationship to the group and to Cindy, Maybonne is aware of its fragility. While she felt and expressed compassion for Cindy's predicament with Doug, she also knows that the rivalry could rear its ugly head at any time. She knows what this tension means even while she worries that she's "being a chump" for letting Cindy think she's "innocent of hatred (which I swear to god *is* my perfect goal)" (p. 95). While Cindy confesses her sins, Maybonne privately reflects on how she didn't like Cindy before and yet how risky it would be to admit that now. "I wished she was my friend, because if Cindy hates you, you don't get invited nowhere" (p. 94).

Now, with Cindy confessing her meanness, Maybonne is reading the situation and struggling to be as ethical as possible. Created within a complex context governed by compulsory heterosexuality, misogyny, and competition for value, two strands of desire operate simultaneously here: One has to do with group association, affirmation, and value, which is structured by threats of violence; and the other is a need to do what's right, to treat others with care expressed in her compassion and goal to be innocent of hatred. This desire is articulated in the choices Maybonne faces in her own self-reflective and critical writing.

The questions that she writes to herself, to her friends, to God, and to Dear Abby, enact a pedagogical translational process with potential to undermine the dominant heterosexist and misogynist processes constructing Maybonne's desire and identity, and to create openings for subjective positions other than subjugated femininity. That is, they are the key to Maybonne's ability to detach, to her becoming educated.

She finds a new attraction, and this time it is David who falls. He becomes too attached to Maybonne, leaving her to wonder again about how this desire thing works: "Brenda told me one time that this thing happens when guys are nice, your feelings can just sort of stop" (p. 100). We are given a glimpse into the operation of a masculine desire that appears not to have the violent, degrading underpinnings related to the mother wound. What I would like to emphasize again here, however, is the way that Maybonne and her friends apply critical insights to their situation. Maybonne is constantly asking what these experiences mean and where they come from. "Marlys Spring" represents the awakening of an ethical "opening out to the world" that occurs through Maybonne's questions, an opening out with the power to shift the hellish experiences she has been living.

As the summer passes, she continues in her friendship with Cindy and goes through one more stint with Doug, who, it seems, has become a "Jesus Freak." She gives both the relationship and the Christian principles a try, but ultimately leaves the new group and Doug. "From the people I met in *One Way* [the Christian group], I feel sorry for Jesus getting stuck with them for worshippers. What a rip" (p. 122).

As she prepares for the first day of school once again, we see that for Maybonne, as for all girls and women, the development of femininity, desire, and identity is contradictory, fraught with tensions and openings, movement in and out of hopeful as well as harmful modes of being and relationship. It is the critical moments when the well-being of oneself and others is questioned and attended to that we see the possibility for more just relationships, identities, and social institutions. These are risky moments, passages toward becoming educated.

Conclusion

As girls round the corner and stumble onto the sexual marketplace, they learn that the stakes are high and the rules are confusing. Girls are caught in a kind of tension among contradictory desires. One is the desire for relationship. Brown and Gilligan (1992) have shown that adolescent girls often give up established relationships—in particular, relationships with other women and girls—as they begin to try to connect themselves with boys, whose developing masculinity keeps in place practices and relations of degradation and violence. It should come as no surprise that in the process, as many studies have shown, girls' self-esteem and academic achievement plummet.

As Simone Weil has taught us, anything that harms the power of thought harms our ability to search for the good, since thought is the source of good. The violent context creating both masculine and feminine desires structured by compulsory heterosexuality, misogyny, and homophobia is certainly harmful to thought. Many girls stop questioning, speaking, and analyzing while in the presence of boys in school classrooms and hallways. But, as I have tried to show here, the construction of femininity is hardly trapped in these processes. Lynda Barry's story of Maybonne in *My Perfect Life* articulates such contradictions. She makes us laugh and cry as we remember with Maybonne the ins and outs, trials and joys of adolescent girlhood. For those of us in teacher education, there is much to be gained from an understanding of the tensions operating around desire, identity, and the politics of compulsory heterosexuality among girls and boys in schools.

Lynda Barry, *My Perfect Life*, p. 127

Moreover, given the kinds of questions that Maybonne poses in her letters and in her journal, what might we learn about the power of such writing, question posing, and interpretation for the ethical development of boys and girls in our own teaching strategies? Maybonne's writing is an active generative process, part of a creative, relational question-posing endeavor that is a source of creation of thinking and thus of all kinds of possibilities. Such question posing, while never simply utopian or predictably positive, is nonetheless the pedagogical source for the generation of a yet-to-come femininity, and the hope for nonviolent, nonmisogynistic, nonhomophobic, nonracist forms of living. In the next chapter, I take up the relationship between this generative force and the power of a recurring ethical question necessary to education as a form of awakening that could alleviate suffering and lead toward a more just world.

Notes

1. When I was a junior at the State University of New York at SUNY Cortland, I had the privilege and good fortune of taking Introduction to Sociology with Dr. Frank Hearn. His critical theory approach to the world blew the lid off for me. From that moment on, all my "big" questions came tumbling out, sometimes at breakneck speed. I am forever grateful to him for that.

2. Drawing on the moral genealogy of German feminist historian Sylvia Bovenschen, Brenkman suggests that the mother/whore representation can be traced to massive social upheavals in the fourteenth and fifteenth centuries when women's prepatriarchal practices and knowledge grounded in the natural world were redefined as black magic, turning some women into witches. The distinction between black magic and white magic allowed women to be categorized as witches or saints. Bovenschen argues that these distinctions form the early patterns that are now experienced psychically and socially as the mother/whore representation.

Chapter 6

Suffering and Social Justice

Teaching in the Passage

Eleven years ago, fresh out of graduate school and driven by a vague yet powerful sense of myself as having something to say about education, I left the security and beauty of my St. Lawrence River home in search of what that something might be. Arriving on the doorstep of Eastern Michigan University, I entered a new passage in my life and found my soul.

I am a teacher educator. I never wanted to be a teacher—quite the contrary, in fact—and yet, while I have had desperate doubts about what I'm doing (am I good enough, do I know enough, are my students committed enough?), I have fallen in love with teaching. Where did this love come from? What is it made of? I love the tension of a good debate, the struggle, the joy, the discomfort, the movement, the questions. I really love the questions. That is what this book has been trying to get at—this love of what goes on between teachers and students, and my faith, my overwhelming loyalty to the creative spirit that is born and plays there in the passage.

Throughout this book, I have been insisting on the need to be aware of two strands of this enterprise, a kind of double dynamic, not unlike falling in love for its startling unpredictability and its persistent hope. One a force, the other an imperative, these strands come together to comprise the unpredictable inventive spirit and the persistent hope of education. The first strand, the creative generative force playing between teachers and students is made because we are relational and translational creatures. We try to make sense of ourselves and others in all kinds of contexts. We ask our questions, we and our students repeat these questions, and thus we invite the play of difference as we create together. Being aware of and attending to this intense, differentiating dynamic requires acknowledging that noisy third person waiting in the wings of all pedagogical relations, inviting her into the room to fling her wild card out into the middle of the conversation, letting the questions and their possible solutions fly into the space and float down between us. It means learning to open to these questions, to expect the discomfort and unpredictability they often bring, their potentially creative or destructive

forces. Such an attention and even affirmation of the power of difference requires patience, learning to be quiet and to wait. This is an active, attentive
waiting, requiring that we relax in the midst of discomfort or difficulty or
chaos, that we learn to appreciate the chaos as an unavoidable, affirmative
force.

The second strand of this dynamic requires bringing a specific question,
the question of well-being, into the space. It means not ignoring the constant
return of the specific ethical question, what is the good? but rather inviting it
to disrupt the complacency of our assumptions and to refigure our life patterns, our relationships with one another and with the Earth. It means paying
attention to the difference made possible by this repetition, even willing it.
How are we to live? What is our responsibility to one another's well-being?
This question demands that we have the courage to make a judgment, to
choose between all the possibilities that might be generated in response to
any question.

To discover oneself in the passage is to discover this double intensity,
the unpredictability of the generative, inventive force of difference coupled
with the hopeful insistence and the interruptive, transformational force of an
ethical question. To live in the intensity of this dynamic is not easy; perhaps
to sustain it is the most difficult task for educators. And yet, what are the
consequences of ignoring or denying either strand? While I have spent con-
siderable time throughout the book teasing out the power of this differentiating force and bringing the ethical question to it, in this chapter I want to
begin with the second strand, this ethical, evaluative imperative. There can
be no education without it, but what does this mean?

The Pedagogy of Suffering

One evening not long ago I dined with a friend. We spoke of epistemol-
ogy, specifically about the differences between positivist perceptions of knowing and what might be called postmodern perspectives. We considered a
number of questions. How is it that we come to know? What role does interpretation and personal interest play? Is objectivity really possible? To what
degree is it possible to discipline the subjective, and so forth. He argued from
the perspective of a rational, unified subject and free will, prioritizing the
individual's capacity to know and make decisions as central to the creation
of culture.

I argued that there were no real or *a priori* foundations for knowing,
that we always bring our values, interests, histories, and so forth to the process of knowing. Moreover, we are collective beings, and some people's
knowledge has historically been seen as more valuable than others'. Hence,

these people, I said, have had the power to control other people's lives in important ways. The quality of people's lives is never simply a matter of an individual's reason or free will. At some point he asked what I thought about the name of my own field of study, Social Foundations. We discussed the problem with the naming of this work that I do as "foundational," and soon after he asked, "How do you decide what is important enough to teach?" A smile came across my face. We had reached the heart of the matter.

Many people suffer the dire consequences of certain definitions of what it means to know, to be human. In all my teaching, what matters most to me is that students begin to grapple with the complex and difficult problem of suffering, in whatever forms or contexts we may encounter it, in order to think about how we should live as humans on this Earth and how we should tend to the lives of other living creatures, human and nonhuman. I do not pretend, nor do I think it is my responsibility, to define what suffering is, either here or in my teaching. Rather, I want my students to learn to grapple with the notion that no matter what perspective(s) we use to answer them, questions of the "good," questions of how we are to live with and treat others, and questions of what and how to teach imply that we awaken to the problem of suffering.

One of the very first principles in the teachings of Buddhism is that life is suffering. The very fact that humans make meaning in and about the world means that we will suffer, for some of this meaning will play negatively upon ourselves and others or will be used to justify harmful acts. This is related to the post-structuralist affirmation of the negative as part of a generative force of difference. If we are to understand fully the productive quality of difference we must understand that it is also creative of that which makes us suffer. It is in how we choose to respond to suffering that determines the quality of our lives.

Some of what we suffer as humans has to do with the sense of incompleteness, loss, dissatisfaction, or confusion that comes through our histories, and with our daily interactions and connections or disconnections with others. Hunger for security or ultimate satisfaction, or the inability to come to grips with the fundamental changeabilty of life causes us to feel pain. Sometimes we get stuck in cycles where we relive or continuously try to resolve these relationships. Buddhists call this form of suffering *dukkha*, and as various forms of psychoanalysis have taught us, much of this form of suffering is of our own making; we make choices and decisions that put us in certain relations that cause us to be off balance or uncentered, and unhappy, even angry. While dukkha is a part of our daily existence, left unattended it can develop into very destructive attitudes and behaviors. As stated by Jungian psychologist Polly Young-Eisendrath,

The human life cycle of birth, development, decline, and death includes much pain and loss that are unavoidable. When understood well, painful experiences awaken us to new meaning and purpose. When dukkha—neurosis or suffering—interferes with our encounters with pain (as it inevitably will), then we are thrown off course in our development, often stuck in self-pity, envy and resentment that lead to more suffering and can even create more pain if we act on them. (1996, p. 13)

Often such discontent and the ways that we choose to cope with dukkha lead to abusive behavior, the effects of which we may not even be aware of. Allowing ourselves to get close to suffering, to lean into its sharp points, as Tibetan monk Chogyam Trungpa Rinpoche teaches, is about becoming awake to it, learning not to run, and learning not to let it fester and become harmful to others. Awakening to suffering (as anger, fear, or resentment) is not really a matter of doing away with it, for that will not happen, but rather a means of learning from it and thus alleviating it in our own lives and the lives of others. To live our lives with this as a central purpose, while understanding that suffering will return with yet another lesson, is to live life ethically, to become educated. Rinpoche's student, Pema Chödrön puts it this way:

Generally speaking, we regard discomfort in any form as bad news. . . . feelings like disappointment, embarrassment, irritation, resentment, anger, jealously, and fear, instead of being bad news, are actually very clear moments that teach us where it is that we're holding back. They teach us to perk up and lean in when we feel we'd rather collapse and back away. They're like messengers that show us with terrifying clarity exactly where we're stuck. This very moment is the perfect teacher, and lucky for us, it's with us wherever we are. (1997, p. 12)

Often we avoid our own suffering or responses to it, and so do not realize the ways we cause harm. Our actions and reactions reverberate onto the world around us, banging into others, sometimes (often) without our noticing or caring to take note. Suffering is never simply an individual experience. "Not causing harm requires staying awake. Part of being awake is slowing down enough to notice what we say and do" (Chödrön, 1997, p. 37).

Of course, most suffering is not consciously of our choosing, but rather is a result of specific structural conditions. Humans, however, are responsible for these phenomena: wars, poverty, violence, corruption, social, political, economic, and ecological injustices. Learning to identify the domain of our responsibility relative to these conditions is certainly part of the process of becoming educated. Personal suffering is created within an institutional and cultural context with specific discernible effects. With my students, I am interested in the ways that suffering can be identified, understood, and alleviated by becoming aware of the psychological, social, and political intricacies surrounding and creating it. When we study homophobia, sexism, racism, or poverty in the schools, for example, we are really looking at how some people are valued less than others, how their interests are considered to be less important, and so how they are made to suffer the often dire consequences of others' prejudicial perspectives and actions. These actions are translated directly into a material reality, a hierarchy of distributed resources (economic, educational, cultural) that leave many people in distress and creating clearly inequitable living conditions: Some people live on the streets and go hungry, while others dine on prime rib in magnificient homes. The inequity is legitimated through a complex, historically constructed ideological system.

This material reality has specific psycholgical consequences as well, that, in turn, affect the abilities of people to respond to their situations or to act in specific ways necessary to change these structures. Richard Sennett and Jonathan Cobb's now classic study, *The Hidden Injuries of Class* (1972), is an excellent, heartrending analysis of the ways our socioeconomic system and the cultural meanings and values supporting it affect the freedom and dignity of those who labor within it, creating "the feeling of not getting anywhere despite one's efforts, the feeling of vulnerability in contrasting oneself to others at a higher social level, the buried sense of inadequacy that one resents oneself for feeling" (p. 58). They later elaborate on the origin of this sense of inadequacy:

> The organization of lives in terms of social production for private profit forms the ground on which the factory, the office, and the school system are organized. . . . Someone is considered "better" both in the sense of competence and in that of having or acting in accordance with higher values; the teachers of the working class with whom we spoke talked about their students as having both less "ability" and "lower" values than others. The uses of ability, of development, of culture, are political questions, questions about which the ruling class in any age sets the standards. . . . this is the ground upon which feelings of inadequacy, as opposed to feelings merely of difference, arise. (pp. 269–270)

More recently, Cornell West has argued that social structures and behavior are inseparable. For West, the idea of structure includes culture and thus goes beyond economic and political organizations to include "families, schools, churches, synagogues, mosques, and communication industries" (1994, p. 19). He goes on to describe the hopelessness and forms of nihilistic behaviors within poor African American communities:

> . . . to talk about the depressing statistics of unemployment, infant mortality, incarceration, teenaged pregnancy and violent crime is one thing. But to face up to the monumental eclipse of hope, the unprecedented collapse of mean-

ing, the incredible disregard for human (especially black) life and property in much of black America is something else. . . . The threat is not simply a matter of economic depression and political powerlessness—though economic well-being and political clout are requisites for meaningful black progress. It is primarily a question of speaking to the profound sense of psychological depression, personal worthlessness, and social despair so widespread in black America. (pp. 19-20)

The system we were born into, live in, and continue to create is founded upon practices and ideologies that value people differently. We can trace specific policies and practices in the schools to the beliefs, attitudes, and actions resulting from such values, and thus key into their harmful effects on the lives of teachers, students, families, and the community.

Sharon Quint's study, *Schooling Homeless Children* (1994), is an excellent example of one principal who woke up to the ways her own actions and the policies of her school were causing great harm to the children of homeless families there. Her compassionate response to that suffering brought the community together in an organized systematic effort to wake up the teachers and community members who, in turn, changed the lives of those children. Attention to such socially, politically, and economically determined forms of suffering with the intention of alleviating it opens one to the other and, as Buddhists argue, is what is required to alleviate our own suffering.

Detachment and Compassion

Simone Weil writes that if we are to be delivered from ourselves we must turn our attention away from ourselves. Detaching from self is a process of considering and responding to the needs of others. While it may be more common to argue that ethical behavior requires detachment from self, Weil looks at the issue from the other direction: Detachment from self, becoming different, requires ethical behavior, that is, attention outside ourselves. As a critical analogy for the notion that we could free ourselves through self-reflection alone, Weil gives the example of the cow who pulls at its hobbles and so falls down (1972, p. 3). While it is certainly necessary to "slow down and recognize what we say and do," we do not become different from ourselves by remaining focused only upon ourselves.

A sense of fullness of life and purpose that will deliver us from our own experiences of dukkha can only be fully developed by engaging others through connection and compassion. Humans are social beings; the meaning we make in and of our lives is created in relation to others, and this includes the meanings that we create around what happiness and goodness are, and with these what suffering is. As soon as we recognize this, we see the play of difference even in the problem of sufering. Unfortunately, though we are nurtured by it, we do not ordinarily recognize the source of our ethical capacity and thus of our own happiness as existing out in the chaotic, difference-bound, changing world itself. This lack of recognition can cause us to stumble and lose our way or get stuck relative to our own becoming educated. As Weil writes,

> The source of man's moral energy is outside himself, like that of physical energy (food, air, etc.). He generally finds it and that is why he has the illusion—as upon the physical plane—that his being carries the principle of its preservation within itself. Privation alone makes him feel his need. (1972, p. 3)

We only move toward the good by recognizing and being awake to suffering, by leaning into it, and this requires considering others' needs by considering and opening to their suffering. Michel Serres writes, "Suffering and misfortune, pain, injustice, and hunger are found at the point where the global touches the local, the universal the singular" (1997, p. 70). It is never simply a matter of individual failing.

Yet, how are we to determine what suffering is or what its relative intensity is in relation to other suffering? Clearly, suffering—or more precisely, our sense of it—is not separate from the same set of interpretive frames that shape our sense of anything else. How we understand it, define it, and attend to it is subject to our individual and collective understanding and the systems that shape such understanding. Suffering is socially constructed, socially understood (or misunderstood) and defined. If we are to use the problem of suffering and the question of well-being as a kind of base for our ethical decision making, we have to be able to engage with others in the determination of what constitutes a form of suffering and what its relation to other forms of suffering is, before we can even begin to address what our response should be. This requires us, as members of any community, to learn to raise the question and to have the courage to propose careful responses. Thus, we invite an inventive spirit; we welcome the playful third; and we practice patience as we listen carefully to the possible answers and learn to wait, to choose carefully together among them.

Sometimes this process itself causes a kind of suffering. The effort to detach from old ideas and behaviors that one might deem to be inappropriate or harmful in some way, may cause pain, discomfort, even trauma. It forces us to confront our own dukkha. Though it may be precisely what is needed to open our hearts, the process of looking at suffering and well-being can cause a form of suffering. The very effort, for example, to look at and grapple with imbedded racist attitudes and behaviors may cause great discomfort and even psychological distress.

Teachers who work to encourage their students (and themselves) to confront ethical questions and to teach others to do so have to be aware of this complex process of detachment. Leaving home is not easy. What kinds of temporary shelter can we provide as our students venture out? What kinds of relational and conceptual security can we provide as they learn to weather the storm brought on by our questions? The point that I'm trying to make, therefore, is that an ethical orientation does not mean doing away with all suffering since some discomfort may be necessary to becoming more caring, careful people. While we must attend to it, suffering has much to teach us. In fact, we must be as conscious of its forms, causes, and effects as possible, willing to deal with what it means in any particular context, and willing to act accordingly in ways that make our lives and the lives of others more purposeful.

Critical Capacities and Compassion

Obviously, the primary question, what is in the best interest of the welfare of this community, is a complex one, dependent upon the ability of the members of the community to communicate their values and decision-making process clearly with each other. This requires critical capacities—the ability to be self-reflective and critical, to pull apart one's thought process and the ideological forms that contribute to it—and communicative competence— the ability to say what we think. Nancy Fraser (1997) examines the debate between critical theorists and post-structuralists around the problem of creating more just social conditions. She contends that the key to an emancipatory politics that takes into consideration the tension (without getting stuck in a false dichotomy) between equality and difference, class politics and cultural politics, and recognizes competing interests and identity differences among people requires just such capacities. Where do these critical capacities come from and what is their relation to an awakening compassion? How are we to understand this necessary ability to ask questions about and propose solutions to injustices if we reject the enlightenment notion that such capacity is essentially internal to us, or "hardwired."

I'm reminded of a colleague's reaction to an early draft of this chapter. Reading my hopeful assertion of the unpredictability circulating within the generative force of difference, he exclaimed, "Well, what would you do when, in the wake of Matthew Shepherd's murder, a student stands up in class and proclaims that all homosexuals are sick and evil, and AIDS is God's way of cleansing the earth of them! How does difference help us out of that one?" Clearly such assertions by students can be heart stopping and are certainly bound to provoke any number of reactions including the desire to impose once again our own assertions of moral law or ontological truth. These painful assertions are filled with indirect, defensive expressions of suffering and often provoke our own fear and anger. Reproducing that anger by insisting on our version of the truth is certainly not going to help the situation. And backing away from the problem, retreating from some students' all-too-familiar retort, "Well, that's *your* opinion," is no better.

My response to my colleague's question is this: "First, can you imagine and accept that such harmful assertions are a sign of the student's own suffering? Can you be compassionate in the face of such an assertion? And second, what form might the compassion take? Specifically, what kinds of questions might you pose to get this student and the class thinking about and responding to the social, historical, and ideological construction of human suffering? What possibilities might circulate in their responses?"

Besides the generally recognized fact that imposing our moral positions on students does little to convince them of any truth (quite the contrary, in fact), this is not our responsibility to them. Rather, I suggest we ask our students to begin to face and challenge the socially formed actions and reactions, and the resulting dukkha, that control their lives and ultimately affect the lives of others. There are simply no easy answers. It is our responsibility (and theirs) to listen carefully and patiently to all the possible responses that come from our pedagogical conversations and to expect the indefinite return of the question. This is the dynamic that teacher education needs to attend to.

Learning to teach, we learn to expect the discomfort that arises as a result of this patience. Teaching in the passage, we learn to attend to, even to will, the constant return of the question of suffering as the means of dealing with and transforming the discomfort. Putting oneself in this difficult passage and struggling with the questions, the uncertainties, and the doubts while we open our hearts to make something new is what it means to fall in love with teaching. And, like any love affair, this is tricky business!

The Transformational Context

Human beings are fundamentally social creatures. We come together from unique places and histories. We depend upon each other for care, for basic needs such as food, shelter, and emotional support and for the development of our particular talents and skills, for the development of our unique contributions to the world. As we enter into social relations, into a socially and discursively organized world or culture, we are shaped and molded by it. The meanings, beliefs, and structures that preexist us have been made historically by just such engagement and are so ingrained in the members of the community or culture as to seem natural.

Nineteenth-century Russian anarchist philosopher Mikhail Bakunin looks carefully at how the sociopolitical and historical context is shot through with the power of a transformational, differentiating force that we both create and are created by. His analysis gets at the social-relational, intergenerational character of the generative force of difference. Put another way, Bakunin analyzes how social life is characterized by complex historical translations that affect who we become. Humans, he writes, are "wholly the product of their history and their environment" (Bakunin, 1953, pp. 152–153). Each individual nature is

> determined by an infinite number of circumstances and conditions preceding the emergence of his will, and which in turn determines his greater or smaller capacity to acquire and assimilate the feelings, ideas and associations worked out by centuries of development and transmitted to everyone as a social heritage by the education which he receives. (p. 153)

Indeed, all of our individual perceiving ability is constructed with this historical context of meanings, beliefs, and interests. Our understanding of ourselves and of the community and the larger world is shaped by this relational context of meaning and the ways that it is exchanged or imposed. All meaning is made within the spaces between us where difference circulates. Reality—and this includes suffering and the sense we make of it—is socially constructed through the very system of differentiation that I have been discussing throughout this book.

It is important here to emphasize the interactive and intersubjective nature of this relational system. As we are shaped and socialized to the given set of meanings and beliefs of any community, we are not passive. We also engage it. We question it, we translate it, we teach it, we paint it, and we shift it collectively. "The infinite diversity of transformation," as Bakunin calls it, or what I have been calling pedagogy is precisely what creates our humanity and connects us to other sentient and nonsentient beings. We encounter it at birth and we live in it and upon it as we engage the world and others who are also created within it.

And though, in the hope of becoming different, we search for how we have become who we are through all of this, the precise weave of this intergenerational, transformational process of becoming is infinitely complex and impossible to trace back precisely. Derrida would add that this impossibility of tracing the origin is not only because of the incredible complexity of history, but also because history and thus culture is a result of mediating formations that create it and give it meaning: we use language to know the world. We interpret the world, and thus interpretation creates the meanings, codes, and ideological maps that make the world sensible to us. And since we do this among a myriad of different historical, familial, and cultural circumstances, in a myriad of differing combinations, our sense of

ourselves and the world we inhabit is fraught with and made of differences.
Bakunin elaborates:

> Differences are determined: Differences among people (races, classes, families)
> are determined by geographic, ethnographic, physiological, and economic
> causes (differences), and also historic, religious, philosophical, juridical, politi-
> cal, and social causes; and all these causes, combined in a manner differing for
> every race, every nation, and more often for every province and every commune,
> for every class and every family, impart to everyone his or her own specific
> physiogamy; that is, a different physiological type, a sum of particular predis-
> positions and capacities independent of the will of the individuals, who are made
> up of them and who are altogether their products. (Bakunin,1953, p. 148)

We actively interact with the beliefs, meanings, symbols, discourses, translations, codes, and systems given to us. We translate. Thus we *participate*, for
better or worse, in the history of its transformation. We read the context, and
as we do, we interpret and necessarily change its meaning. But, in what ways?
For what purposes? And how conscious are these shifts we enact? How awake
to them or their effects are we?

Of course, schooling is positioned precisely in the middle of the translational process. Schools are clearly vehicles of cultural transmission tied to
political and economic interests; they are ideological state apparatuses as
Althusser (1971) taught us years ago. Teachers' particular ideological maps,
their individual and collective histories, and their desires are all implicated in
this institutional dynamic.

A discussion of critical capacities that does not fall into a dependence
upon the rational atomized individual, some predetermined essential ability,
or to *a priori* notions of history as foundational takes this translational, inventive, socializing context into account. And this includes both the happiness and suffering that is created there, a complex task for sure.

This flexion of cultural forces and inventive processes is part and parcel
of how we come to be thinking, teaching, inventing, dancing, writing human
beings. It actually shapes what it means to think. And while it is certainly transformational, this is not necessarily a "progressive" process. As I have said, there
is nothing inherently "good" in any of the inventive relations that we engage.
This means that we must ask a fundamental question and be willing to recognize its perpetual repetitive function in our lives. This question is simply, What
is the good for this community?

Of course, it is not a simple endeavor to engage it. It requires a tremendous amount of critical self-reflection and the willingness to recognize and
detach from imbedded beliefs and psychological attachments, again and again.
Moreover, it requires that we also turn that critique outward to how the structures, relations, and beliefs in our communities and cultures impede, harm,

or serve us, and what we believe needs to change. This clearly requires a collective conversation that not only includes teachers but is their special domain. It requires a collective ethical conversation, including the ability to recognize both one's own ideological predispositions and those taken by others, to analyze existing relations, and to communicate effectively as we interpret, invent, and choose new possibilities. This is where the hope lies. Trying to make it happen is mind boggling and complicated, but why else teach? Understanding this is why I love what I do.

My argument assumes that, along with suffering, freedom and autonomy are shaped within and are contingent upon a given context. Our ability to be free and our understanding of the concomitant responsibilities in the face of suffering are created in relation to others within this socially constructed, intersubjective, translational system. This understanding calls into question idealist notions of autonomy that view individual free will to be the source for freedom external of any influence from the given context or historical forces (Bakunin, 1953; Bowers, 1984; Greene, 1988). It also calls into question the notion that there is a foundational model, telos, or *a priori* foundational principles to guide us in our decisions about how to make the world a better, safer place. Freedom lies in the recognition of the creative possibilities born from our ability to think collectively about the world, coupled with the desire to sustain life by addressing that which threatens it.

Again, it is the specific interminable question of how we could alleviate the suffering of others that offers us the gift of both personal and social transformation. But we must understand that there is no final or certain answer to this question. Our ability to ask and to pose answers, and the courage to face the question all over again, are created within the transformational context that we share with each other. Critical capacities are possible precisely because of the generative force of difference created socially, not in spite of it, and our well-being depends upon the strength and courage of the resulting evaluations. I return to a passage from Deleuze, which I shared in Chapter 1:

> The problem of critique is that of the value of values, of the evaluation from which their value arises, thus the problem of their creation. *Evaluation is defined as the differential element of corresponding values, an element which is both critical and creative.* Evaluations in essence are not values but ways of being, modes of existence of those who judge and evaluate, serving as principles for the values on the basis of which they judge. This is why we always have the beliefs, feelings and thoughts that we deserve given our way of being and our style of life. (1983, p. 1)

Difference generates value and the evaluations of value, and all the attending attitudes, actions, perspectives, and questions. And this is why pedagogy and the critical questions that we bring to the resulting possibilities are so important and so intertwined. Again, the "good" is nothing more or less than the result of our singular and collective translational efforts around its infinite definition. When we turn to education, to our desire to become different from who we have been relative to the presence of suffering, we bring our questions, our judgments, and our evaluative capacities to all the possibilities generated in our relationships to each other. We awaken our hearts to what others suffer, we respond, and thus we relieve our own pain.

Moving Toward Grace

Agreeing with others within the Buddhist tradition, Young-Eisendrath writes that it is unlikely that most of us will ever be completely free from suffering, yet we can reach a

> condition in which we reap the benefits of suffering, in which we come to understand how suffering can be alleviated, and how pain can be transformed into compassion and development. Suffering is useful and not merely a waste of time, when it awakens us to our responsibility for our own attitudes and thoughts and actions. Within suffering are the gifts of self-awareness and compassion. (1996, p. 32)

Perhaps we could say that the possibility for critical capacities that could transform our world is generated within a pedagogy of suffering, within educational relations that take suffering on as a central transformational question. With self-awareness and compassion comes the ability to change one's own life and also to contribute to transforming communities. In considering suffering, facing it with others, seeking a response to its various forms, we necessarily engage the generative force of difference, and thus we create passages to other ways of living, of being.

As Simone Weil teaches, if we create in such a way as to sustain life, we move toward grace. To move toward grace is to recognize and accept both the *responsibility* to alleviate suffering and the *impossibility* of ultimately ending it. There are no final answers, just the interminable return of questions and the empty limit space of their potential answers. There is nothing to reach but the return of this void and our own limits in the face of it. "Grace fills empty spaces but it can only enter where there is a void to receive it, and it is grace itself that makes the void." (Weil, 1972, p. 10)

A commitment to be awake to the meanings that suffering can have requires a commitment to the infinite fullness of and indefinite movement of thought, a will to truth and the good that recognizes the productive power of the limit space, the ultimate unanswerability of our questions. Because humans are imperfect, we can never finally arrive at the good; it will always appear to be just out of reach. This is often disconcerting and painful, but the good is also constituted by this understanding of groundlessness and cannot be reached without it.

Thoroughly immersed in pedagogy, teachers thus have an enormous responsibility and opportunity to encourage students' own engagement and creative potential and their concomitant critical ethical capacities. And what joy there is in this endeavor, powerful enough to take our hearts! Powerful enough to awaken us to the alleviation of suffering in the lives of others. Yes, there are an infinite number of possibilities and even more questions, but still, how are we to live?

Chapter 7

Earth, Ethics, and Education

A frog is no less alive than we are. To think so and to act so is one of the gravest dangers to life.
—Susan Chernak McElroy

Reverence for life comprises the whole ethic of love in its deepest and highest sense.
—Albert Schweitzer

My mother's mother died when she was an infant. She grew up on a dairy farm in the St. Lawrence River valley of northern New York with three older sisters, an older brother, and my grandfather who never got over the loss of his wife Jesse. When asked who raised her, my mom has been known to say, "the horses," and I have always delighted in hearing that. Conjured up in my mind are images of tiny Frannie Brown, atop one of my grandfather's gentle Percheron giants, off to fetch the cows. In a photo album found among her recently deceased sister's posessions, there she is, my mom at age five or so, sitting in the yard with her elbow propped against a big German shepherd as though the two were just hanging out enjoying each other's company on a hot summer afternoon. Under the picture is scrawled, "Frances Brown and her dog Betty." Seeing this picture for the first time, I swear my heart came undone.

Something very old washed over me, something primary in my own particular history that has to do with my own love for horses and dogs, trees and meadows. The sudden understanding that my mother first brought to me this intense love for—even friendship with—nonhuman creatures and the Earth wells up in my throat, and even as I try to write this now, I am overcome by it.

Thinking about this, I realize that much of what I do in my life personally and professionally is directly tied to that intergenerational love, and yet I have never really looked at it, or written about it, or taught about it carefully enough. This includes the associated pain I feel in the face of the desperate situation we've brought the Earth to. Some kind of strange embarrassment hangs around this sense of myself as having such strong heart-ties to animals, forests, rivers, and lakes. One can *feel* that way, one can love one's dogs or really dig old trees, but bring it into a teacher education classroom? I am beginning to understand this denial in my own life as constructed within a powerful sociosymbolic system in this culture that devalues nonhuman species, cares less for them, attends less, and thus is willing to destroy them. This chapter brings the pedagogy of suffering introduced in the previous chapter to a discussion of our relationship with the Earth and the associated responsibility we have as educators to open our hearts to the questions related to our own interdependence with the complex life forms we live among.

Each semester I ask my undergraduates, eager to become teachers, to struggle with the question, What does it mean to become educated? Most respond that it means learning to survive, to get jobs, to learn to get along, to cope. A few gesture toward making the world a better place through attention to diverse cultures and people, but only a few. And it is very rare that a student offers the idea that an educated person would be committed to caring for the Earth. I wonder about this, and I wonder too why it has taken me so long to come home to this question: What is the relation between Earth, ethics, and education?

Awe and Interbeing

Thinking about how to get started, I've been flooded with memories of my childhood and especially of time spent with my mother: Walking through the woods with all its pungent earth smells and sweet bird and wind sounds, Mom bent to identify the tiniest, most delicate plants, never picking, just looking, admiring. Or riding horseback through a field, smelling clover and wild things, hot sun on our backs, deer flies buzzing and biting, she taught me to listen to the horse with my hips and thighs, to talk respectfully to him with my hands and calves. Without ever saying so, my mother taught me to love my own bodily connection with the Earth and animals as a means of respect, care, and joy. Quite simply, she taught me this as the only means of living myself.

I remember being filled with a kind of awe just at being in the middle of a meadow on a trip to pick wild flowers for her. All those varieties of flowers and plants: Queen Anne's lace, vetch, daisies, chickory, and thistle. All the bugs buzzing, and the hot sun warming me: here they were again, the same crazy combination as last year, and yet never the same. With or without me or anyone, here they all were again, all this beautiful life. This is what people must mean by God, I thought. And there I was again too, happy and at ease amongst it all.

Since I grew up this way, it makes sense to me to think of humans as simply living among all this buzzing diversity, separate but not separate, other and not other, a particular development within the seemingly infinite possibilities offered by whatever complex of forces make things live. Vietnamese Buddhist monk Thich Nhat Hanh calls this sense of life "interbeing endlessly interwoven":

> All phenomena are interdependent. When we think of a speck of dust, a flower, or a human being, our thinking cannot break loose from the idea of unity, of one, of calculation. But if we truly realize the interdependent nature of the dust, the flower and the human being, we see that unity cannot exist without diversity. Unity is diversity, and diversity is unity. This is the principle of interbeing. (1993, p. 129)

What we refer to as nature is really nothing more or less than all of the existing and possible relations, transformations, and developments that make up "life." And we humans cannot possibly understand or know completely and finally how it all works, precisely because it is not stable. This is where the awe lies for me, in all the interconnected variety and unrestrainable growing and changing. How incredibly rich and wonderful!

I am reminded of a passage in a beautiful novel by Anne Roife, who exalts the life of the sea in a similar way:

> Mid stride, awe caught. It mingled with a joy that would not be still. Tenderness spilled over the wave chasing her ankles, tenderness for the glory of the infinite crab legs under the shifting sand, the pocked sand itself, the mound of mollusk and fish, eyeball and scale. She considered the millions of parasites that lived in the clumps of seaweed attached to the drying log ahead. Their shape and their appetites came sharply, individually to her mind: awe. (1993, pp. 5–6)

That is in part what I want to explore in this chapter, this disappearing sense of exaltation, of love and tenderness, and compassion for this awesome Earth and our places within its vast web of life. I will argue that the inability to recognize our interbeing with other nonhuman species is created within specific economic, scientific, cultural, and ideological conditions. With the expansion of a global economic agenda, the human population is intensifying a hyperseparated relation with the Earth. This is an ideological, emotional, and discursive disconnection necessary to an industrial and now postindustrial economic system. It prevents us from recognizing our immersion in, participation in, and dependence upon a vast transformative process creating both culture and the nonhuman beings we are bent on destroying.

Understanding the interdependence between cultural forms and ecological conditions requires an awakening to the awesome beauty and integrity of nonhuman life forms and is key to the survival of the Earth (Bowers, 1997). It requires that we understand the suffering that our denial and disconnection impose. With education, the dynamic relation between difference and ethics, lies the hope of bringing back the awe, compassion, and love necessary to our survival on this living, breathing Earth.

Eco-erosic Love

Curriculum theorist Susan Edgerton calls this love "eco-erosic." "That is," she writes, drawing on Michel Serres, "love of the land (local) and of the earth (global). Love of one's neighbors and intimates (local) and love of humankind (global) cannot be separated from one another, or from love of land and earth, 'under penalty of hatred'" (Edgerton, 1996, p. 70). Serres insists that love is not the opposite of hatred, for hatred is the sum of all contraries (1989, p. 83). Hatred separates and excludes; but as Edgerton says, "love pays attention" (p. 69), perhaps especially to that which history would exclude and thus cause to suffer.

This is the love that my mother tended to with me. Without calling it that, she taught me to pay careful attention to the details of the forest floor and the horse's sensibilities as a means of connecting and of opening my heart to the suffering of nonhuman creatures. And now, I'm writing to ask, what connects us in love with the Earth and her creatures, and why does it seem so difficult in this postindustrial world to awaken such love?

I write, in part, because I suffer badly, perhaps excessively, in the face of nonhuman creature suffering. I confess that this pain is often worse than what I experience in the face of human pain. I can't stand it. And yet, I'm certain that this suffering has led me down the path that I have chosen, to study education as a means of alleviating suffering, as a means toward the awakening of compassion. As I argued in the previous chapter, this is what ethics means, a willingness to look suffering in the face in order to relieve it in whatever ways possible, to awaken our hearts to a compassion for others that will ultimately save ourselves. In this chapter, I bring this notion of ethics squarely into the middle of an ecological crisis, to consider what such a commitment to understand suffering might mean for the ways we think about and the ways we interact with others on this Earth.

Over the last 10 years or so, I've pursued that path, thinking about human lives and education's relation to questions of *social* justice. Against a view of education that is primarily technical and strives to present us with instrumentalized methods leading to predictable, controllable outcomes, I am writing about the teaching-learning relation as a set of actions and reactions, communications and translations generating transformations that are both infinite in their possibility and unforeseeable or unpredictable in their effects. Pedagogy, the dynamic relation between teachers and students, generates a powerful array of responses and effects. But, it is education as the attention to both to this differentiating process and its effects, including those effects that may cause suffering, that turns us toward an ethical response, that is, toward a willingness to attend generously to the other.

Now in a circular way I come back to what my mother taught me first, to think about what it could mean to be compassionate and generous and openhearted in our relation with the Earth and her creatures. I want to examine questions relative to ethics and the Earth, and I ask that teachers and teacher educators begin to understand and attend to our critical places within this process. We in teacher education are beginning to think carefully about and teach our students the necessity of a commitment to the politics of human diversity, but we have largely ignored the politics of biodiversity and the massive suffering that we as humans continue to cause the Earth and ultimately ourselves.

Hyperseparation and Suffering

Stephen J. Gould has written that we are unlikely to protect that which we do not love (quoted in Smith & Williams, 1998, p. 7). Perhaps we could extend his sentiment by saying that we are unlikely to protect that which we fear or that which we believe necessary to our economic or cultural survival and thus fundamentally exploitable. We are facing a very fragile earthly condition where species after species is disappearing as we cut down their habitats or pollute their waters for our own growth "needs." Just look out the window the next time you're in a jet, flying cross-country. The grid of human development and the consequent loss of forests is devastating. And yet, our own survival is at stake because, for the most part, we are not teaching our children to love and respect the very ground that supports their bodies or the trees that produce the air filling their lungs. Or perhaps more accurately, we have become alienated from the child's sense of awe at and interbeing with this life-giving and beautiful Earth. That alienation is somewhat understandable when thought of in light of our historical need to survive. But it is time to awaken our hearts and minds to an understanding that our own well-being is dependent upon the love and exhaltation, the nurturing of that which, in our vulnerability, we once feared and now in arrogance simply forget.

Cultural geographers urge us to think about the ways that we weave our identities in relation to the landscape. We make our homes and raise our families, we work and play within those spaces. We anchor ourselves in and traverse the Earth. Yet, somehow these corporal and psychological connections are largely lost to consciousness or denied through layers of ideological messages that claim human superiority to and radical exclusion from nature. We have become radically disconnected or "hyperseparated" from an understanding of our interconnection with and interdependence upon all the forces of life itself. We have built urban fortresses against such an understanding, and many children grow up with no opportunity to love the Earth, to stand in awe of her insects, her dogtooth violets, her marsh cattails, bears, rivers, canyons, and meadows. Our history is creating a tragedy for our children, all the children of the Earth, indeed all Earth's creatures, since all human and nonhuman suffering is interconnected. Fritjof Capra puts it this way:

> The more we study the major problems of our time, the more we come to realize that they cannot be understood in isolation. They are systemic problems, which means that they are interconnected and interdependent. For example, stabilizing world population will be possible only when poverty is reduced worldwide. The extinction of animal and plant species on a massive scale will continue as long as the Southern Hemisphere is burdened by massive debts. Scarcities of resources and environmental degradation combine with rapidly expanding populations to lead to the breakdown of local communities and to the ethnic and tribal violence that has become the main characteristic of the post–cold war. (1996, pp. 3–4)

We live oblivious or indifferent to both the suffering and the life forces within and between these things, as though the living things around us were mere objects for our use and disposal, and not essential to our own lives and survival, or even more importantly, not having any integrity of their own, autonomous of human needs. Too many of us live in a strange illusion that there is no reason to care if a tree gets cut down, or a possum hit in the road. Chainsaw roar and roadkill are just rubble and background noise in the hubbub of modern life.

A recent experience demonstrates. A friend and I were in the nursery section of a large home improvement store and heard something cheeping. Several newborn baby birds had fallen out of their nest onto the concrete below. They were barely alive, dehydrated, and desperately trying to chirp. I gathered them up, hailing a young woman clerk for help. She said rather monotonously, "Oh, yeah. The birds. They keep falling out of their nest," and, upon my repeated request, went to look for a box. A young man walking by, looked at us and said, shrugging, "Hey. That's nature," and continued on his way. I was assaulted by the indifference, and the birds were dying of dehydration.

The idea that it's "nature" and therefore not our responsibility has its roots in a long history of Western thought from Plato through Bacon and Descartes, and beyond. Many ecofeminists, ecologists, and philosophers have documented the development of a dualist way of thinking that separates human culture from nature and hierarchizes the pair, endowing humans with the right to mastery. Feminists link the mastery of nature to the domination of women who are seen historically as less rational, reproductive servants, akin to the Earth and therefore in need of a master.

Ecofeminist philosopher Val Plumwood writes a thorough and convincing critique of the dualistic structure of Western thought and the "backgrounding" of nonhuman life forms, which has historically created hyperseparated human identities. That is, we define ourselves consciously and unconsciously through discourses and practices that radically separate us from and "background" nonhuman forms of life. At best, nature is seen in this thought as the mere backdrop or stage for the enactment of human desires, needs and actions.

> The biosphere forms the taken for granted material substratum of human existence, always present, always functioning, always forgiving; its needs do not have to be considered, just as the needs of other species generally do not have to be considered, except as they occasionally impinge upon or threaten the satisfaction of our own. Systematic devaluation and denial are perceptually ingrained in backgrounding, involving not noticing, not seeing. (1993, p. 70)

This way of being that endows nature with only a use value is produced through a taken-for-granted binary structure of thought thousands of years in the making. In Plato's philosophy, for example, the ideal world of Forms is held as the most valuable and desirable realm over and above the natural earthly world of Appearances. Through an engagement with reason, humans are to aspire to the divine world of ideal beauty and good, leaving behind apparent earthly beauty and pleasures associated with the body. Plato writes in the *Phaedo* (267-269) as follows:

> if the nature of man could sustain the sight, he would acknowledge that this other world was the place of the true heaven and the true light and the true earth. For our earth, and the stones, and the entire region which surrounds us, are spoilt and corroded, as in the sea all things are corroded by brine, neither is there any perfect or noble growth, but caverns only, and sand, and an endless sough of mud; and even the sore is not to be compared to the fairer sights of this [other] world. And still less is this our world to be compared to the other. (quoted in Plumwood, 1993, p. 96)
>
> Plato goes on to describe the rich colors of the other world: they are brighter far and clearer than ours; there is a purple of wonderful lustre, also the radiance of gold and the white which is in the earth is whiter than any chalk or snow. . . . The reason is that they are pure, and not like our precious stones, infected or corroded by the corrupt briny elements which coagulate among us,

and breed foulness and disease both in the stones as well as in animals and plants. (quoted in Plumwood, 1993, p. 97)

Thus, in Platonic thought as in Christianity, the meaning of life and death for humans is to be found elsewhere, not in the Earth or in human life as part of nature, but in a separate realm accessible only to chosen humans through the world of Forms and heaven (Plumwood, 1993, p. 100). Privileging the world gained through reason over "corrupt" nature and the body, Plato subjects all nonhuman creatures and some humans to a second class status and ultimately to a logic of the master.

Peter Coates, in his comprehensive study of Western attitudes on nature since ancient times, discusses the theological debates relative to the interpretation of Christian doctrine on the nonhuman world, especially interpretations of Genesis. He concludes that the dominant perspective gleaned from interpretations of the Bible is that "man," exclusively endowed with a soul, is granted dominion over the earth. Yet, Coates also recognizes the "green gloss put on many medieval religious ideas by theologians," especially those adhering to a view of human stewardship for nature. He discusses fifteenth-century trials whereby whole groups of animals or insects were publicly accused *and defended* for their crimes against human culture. In a hilarious passage, Coates gives the example of a certain Pierre Rembaud who made his reputation in France defending a variety of creatures' God-given right to "have suitable and sufficient means of support" since "everything that creepeth upon the earth, every green herb has been given for meat" (1998, p. 51).

In addition to these stories of medieval translations of God's law that grant to animals and other nonhuman species human "rights," Coates also refers to Pope John Paul II's unprecedented 1989 environmental address discussing ozone layer and rain forest depletion. Clearly, like any ideological body, Christianity has been the object of a myriad of interpretive efforts. Nonetheless, Coates argues, the dominant Christian tradition echoing the ancient perspectives legitimates "wanton exploitation of nature" as a human perogative.

> Notwithstanding the imagination and resourcefulness that early animal defence lawyers and recent ecotheologians have demonstrated in their efforts to reinterpret Genesis and to identify and resurrect marginal and forgotten aspects of the Christian tradition, the most influential interpretation has been despotic. In this respect, early Christian theologians reinforced the existing logic of a dualism that downgraded the physical environment and enshrined the spiritual. (Coates, 1998, p. 52)

Coates, Plumwood, and others (Abram, 1996; Capra, 1982, 1996; Harvey, 1996; Singer, 1993, 1995) trace this dualism through Bacon and into Descartes, emphasizing the Cartesian "apartheid between spirit, mind, and culture on the one hand and matter, body and nature on the other" (Coates, 1998, p. 75). Well-known from his *Discourse on Method*, Descartes's hierarchy of mind over matter (body and nature) argues for the complete legitimation of the manipulation of the inferior body by a superior mind. Descartes practiced anatomical experimentation on animals without anesthetic, demonstrating his belief that nonhuman species did not suffer the likes of human pain. Animal rights activist Peter Singer has decried the Cartesian likening of animals to machines as a critical moment in the overwhelming destruction of the non-human world of the last two centuries.

Clearly, this ideological development is woven through the development of capitalism and the increasing demands for raw resources needed to produce and accumulate wealth. The expense to the earth and nonhuman life forms, as well as to the human lives whose labor converts these resources to profit for others, is simply overlooked in favor of individual human prosperity and success. Clearly a redefinition of these terms, *prosperity* and *success*, is needed if we are to survive. Without a strong ethical stand that focuses upon the protection of ecological diversity and the sustainability of human life in careful balance with other life forms, we are certainly doomed to destroy ourselves.

For Singer, the principle of equal consideration of interests at the heart of his utilitarian view of ethics is measured through a consideration of suffering, and while he looks carefully at gender and race as categories of human equality, his perspective includes nonhuman species as well. In considering our long history of speciesism as part of our hyperseparated ideological structures, Singer notes some alternative perspectives, including the view of Jeremy Bentham writing at the turn of the nineteenth century:

> The day may come when the rest of the animal creation may acquire those rights which could never have been withholden from them but by the hand of tyranny. The French have already discovered that the blackness of the skin is no reason why a human being should be abandoned without redress to the caprice of a tormentor. It may one day come to be recognized that the number of legs, the villosity of the skin, or the termination of the *os sacrum*, are reasons equally insufficient for abandoning a sensitive being to the same fate. What else is it that should trace the insuperable line? Is it the faculty of reason, or perhaps the faculty of discourse? But a fullgrown horse or dog is beyond comparison a more rational, as well as more conversable animal, than an infant of a day, or a week, or even a month, old. But suppose they were otherwise, what would it avail? The question is not, Can they *reason?* not Can they *talk?* but *Can they suffer?* (quoted in Singer, 1993, pp. 56-57)

As indicated by Bentham, the history of Western philosophy and science has been composed of efforts to "prove" our human superiority over nature through observations of the "obvious inferiority" of other creatures due to their varying degrees of lack (lack of vertebrae, lack of language, lack of speech, lack of mind), and our abilities to interpret and control natural "laws." We use our capacities for language and representation to produce hierarchy after hierarchy, grouping after grouping, thus deciding where every sentient and nonsentient creature fits under our system. Such "natural" hierarchies make it possible not to perceive nonhuman others (or human others) as suffering from our selfish actions. They are, after all, where they belong.

As contemporary inhabitants of Western culture, we have been born into and socialized by a complex system of belief, practice, and habit that denies the autonomous integrity of the nonhuman world, as well as our interdependence with nonhuman others, keeping our human identities hyperseparated from this backgrounded "other world." This dualized self arrogantly assumes itself to be the center and master of the universe, in need of no one, independent. Autonomy and morality in this perspective are internal, God-given, and independent of anyone or anything else except as these might serve individual needs. Sustained by such divine omnipotence, this self-centered individual is free to exploit that which he needs to prosper (Bakunin, 1953, pp. 122–125). Arguing that "the hyperseparated self can have no basis or reason to empathize with the other or to consider the other as more than the instrument of its independently defined needs," Plumwood quotes Walter Benjamin:

> The dualised self which can only view nature instrumentally cannot recognize in nature another who is both different from self and non-alien, and misses the essential tension of recognizing the outside other as both different and alike. (Plumwood, 1993, p. 157)

Obviously, industrial capitalism, framed by free-market principles and associated ideas within classical liberalism, developed through this ideological climate. The Earth and her creatures have become resources to be exploited and turned into consumable profit-making objects. The ideology and habit of hyperseparation allows us to objectify, manipulate, and control nature's creatures in the name of human knowledge, need (read consumption), and rights.

In tandem with these economic developments, modern science orders the disorderly world, influencing social policy and technological innovation, legitimating through "knowledge" and "reason," human domination over natural forces.

> Indeed, the ostensibly "value-free" results of our culture's investigations into biology, physics, and chemistry ultimately come to display themselves in the open and uncertain field of everyday life, whether embodied in social policies

> with which we must come to terms or embodied in new technologies with
> which we all must grapple. (Abram, 1996, p. 34).

In our technologically driven daily lives, baby birds dying of dehydration on
a concrete floor are just "nature." We are convinced that our technological
and instrumental forms are the way to a better life, which turns out to be a
life of superconsumption, making both human and nonhuman suffering easy
to ignore, or not see at all. We have taxonomies and categories designating
where everything under the sun "belongs," allowing us to forget, as Thich
Nhat Hahn says, that "the sun is our heart."

> We know that if our heart stops beating, the flow of our life will stop, but we
> do not take the time to notice the many things outside of our bodies that are
> equally essential for our survival. . . . If the sun were to stop shining, the flow
> of our life would stop. The sun is our second heart, our heart outside our body.
> It gives all life on Earth the warmth necessary for existence. Plants live thanks
> to the sun. Their leaves absorb the sun's energy, along with carbon dioxide from
> the air, to produce food for the tree, the flower, the plankton. And thanks to
> plants, we and other animals can live. . . . We cannot begin to describe all the
> effects of the sun, that great heart outside our body. (1993, p. 128)
>
> Our Earth, our green beautiful Earth is in danger, and all of us know it.
> Yet, we act as if our daily lives have nothing to do with this situation of the world.
> If the Earth were your body, you would be able to feel many areas where she is
> suffering. (p. 132)

Such forgetting of our interbeing with all other living things perpetuates
an inability to come to terms with the massive harm that our technologies
and hyperseparated experiences of ourselves cause to other living beings as
well as to ourselves. We are blocked from the ability to open to suffering created through this hyperseparation, and our own well-being and survival is
clearly at grave risk. Such denial blocks our ability to think about ways of
encouraging sustainability in balance with the Earth's resources and nonhuman
creatures. As American ecofeminist and spiritualist, Starhawk writes:

> If we weren't living in a state of denial all the time, the whole idea of sustainability
> would clearly be our first priority. How is it that we can live in a world where
> we use the Earth in ways that are destroying it and not worry? We all know we
> have to breathe; we all know we have to drink water; we all know we have to
> eat food; and, we all know it's got to come from somewhere. So why isn't the
> preservation of the environment our first priority? It makes such logical sense
> that it's irritating to have to say it. (1995, p. 277)

Sustainablility, it seems to me, depends upon an understanding of the moving energy and interconnection between all life forms, an acceptance of
interbeing.

Difference and Unity, Awe and Exhaltation

In this project, I've been searching for writings that recognize the un-knowable and respect the awesome difference-producing forces in the world, as a source for generating attention to and responsibility for what we do on this Earth. I am moved by views of the world that seek to understand, while letting the mystical in, the strangeness, the moving unknowable.

I have found an overwhelming body of literature with perspectives as varied as philosophy and the social and natural sciences themselves. I'm drawn to literary pieces that express visions marginalized by the dominance of hier-archical systems. They move me for their expressions of eco-erosic love. In *The Education of Little Tree* (1976), for example, Forrest Carter writes beau-tifully of a young Cherokee boy's loving, learning relationship with the life of a mountain. Here Little Tree recalls a spring storm:

> Then it comes again and rolls blue fireballs off rocks on the ridge tops and splat-ters the blue in the air. The trees whip and bend in the sudden rushes of wind, and the sweep of heavy rain comes thunking from the clouds in big drops, let-ting you know there's some real frog-strangling sheets of water coming close behind.
>
> Folks who laugh and say that all is known about Nature, and Nature don't have a soul spirit, have never been in a mountain spring storm. When she's birthing spring, she gets right down to it, tearing at the mountains like a birthing woman clawing at the bed quilts. (p. 102)

I am moved by forms—writing or sculpture, cinema or dance—that strive to acknowledge and translate this awesome life force. As pointed out by Grandma in Carter's tale, such an acknowledgment is part of the development of the "spiritmind," that part of our humanity that learns to open to and care for the lives of others as we pursue our own happiness. For Little Tree, these others are both human and nonhuman others. As Starhawk writes, such an under-standing of our interconnectedness calls us "to a politics and set of actions that come from compassion, from the ability to literally feel with all living beings on the Earth" (1995, p. 275). Clearly, our very survival on this earth compels us toward such a politics. And such a politics depends upon an edu-cation, including teacher education, that awakens us to interbeing and to compassion.

I am troubled, however, by works among ecological theorists, artists, and enthusiasts that endow nonhuman forces or creatures with human character-istics. While I understand why we might be drawn to do so, to use our own experiences to describe the other, I find the endowment of the wind or a mountain with anthropomorphic qualities untenable and unconvincing. Giv-ing a tree or a stone, for example, qualities of mind is not only unconvincing, it denies important differences and reproduces the misguided and dangerous notion that mind—and thus humanity—is a superior form. I have been frustrated with those overromanticized writings that, in their noble desire to value the Earth, insist upon doing so through what we have traditionally valued most—ourselves!

Within a diverse body of literary, philosophical, ecological, and scientific work interested in attending to our responsibility of interbeing on this Earth is the shared idea that we are both different and not separate from the vast and complex life forces into which we are born and ultimately return in death. To understand human suffering created within complex social relations and culture, we must grasp the ways that human culture is created within the larger web of life. Suffering creates suffering, and must be addressed as such. This is where education intersects with the differential force of pedagogy.

In the Introduction to this book, I wrote that I feel the world in my body as an affirmative force; I am touched and moved by the creative, generative forces that surround us all the time, and I am certain that our pedagogical activities are part of these forces. My childhood sense of awe and exaltation for the living, changing integrity and beauty of the natural world and my desire to address our connection to it, indeed, our construction within it, was unexpectedly reawakened by my discovery of the philosophy of Mikhail Bakunin. While Bakunin's work is clearly limited by particular nineteenth-century concepts, his ideas pertaining to the complex generative forces running through both human and nonhuman life and the simultaneous diversity and unity of the forces and forms within this system echo both the Buddhist and ecological ideas that I have been looking at, as well as specific ideas about difference within post-structuralism. His writings unpack, with a unique clarity, the relationship between difference and unity.

> Nature is the sum of actual transformations of things that are and will ceaselessly be produced within its womb. Whatever exists, all the beings which constitute the undefined totality of the Universe, all things existing in the world, whatever their particular nature may be in respect to quality or quantity—the most diverse and the most similar things, great or small, close together or far apart—necessarily and unconsciously exercise upon one another, whether directly or indirectly, perpetual action and reaction. All this boundless multitude of particular actions and reactions, combined in one general movement, produces and constitutes what we call Life, Solidarity, Universal Causality, Nature. Call it, if you find it amusing, God, the Absolute—it really does not matter—provided you do not attribute to the word God a meaning different from the one we have just established: the universal, natural and necessary and real but in no way predetermined, preconceived or foreknown combination of the infinity of particular actions and reactions which all things having real existence incessantly exercise upon one another.

. . . It creates and will always be created anew; it is the combined unity, everlastingly created by the infinite totality of the ceaseless transformations of all existing things; and at the same time it is the creator of those very things; each point acts upon the Whole and the Whole acts upon every point. (Bakunin, 1953, p. 263)

When I first read this, I thought, "My goodness! Bakunin is writing about pedagogy!" As the essays I've presented throughout this book argue, pedagogical relations produce these same kinds of actions and reactions, creating multiple effects including those we need to change the world. I've thought about this process in terms of choreography; I've looked at it as analogous to translation; I've even thought about it as a kind of nomadic process, as leaving home; but these are all social processes. Bakunin uses this same sense to write about the entirety of life forces, the social and the natural as one unified, universal set of forces creating all the possible diverse forms known and unknown.

According to Bakunin, the social cannot be separated off from the natural, since they are part of the same "universal solidarity." The solidarity that Bakunin refers to is a process, a transformative life process that cannot, he argues, be isolated within "nature" or excluded from what is human. This indefinite, transformative, ultimately creative relation, is actually part of the same force that produces itself anew in each successive moment, that is never the same, that creates life itself.

Reading this practically knocked me off my chair. No wonder I have been attracted to the pedagogical relation and have been compelled to articulate its fundamental generative process—this is the process that has awed me all my life about the world, about life itself!

Again, the argument that I am trying to make by introducing Bakunin's work is that as humans, we are part of a set of creative, dynamic forces—a "universal solidarity" to use Bakunin's words—and even those relations and processes that seem to us to be uniquely human processes (reason and thus pedagogy, for example) have similar generative forces in operation that can be found in the larger world around us. What is understood to be "universal" here is not a determining final truth about what it means to be human or nonhuman, but rather a dynamic, transformative force that makes final answers impossible. Taking such a notion of transformative, dynamic, interbeing seriously, one cannot so easily exclude and inferiorize the natural world and its "laws" from our own lives.

Moreover, if this is so, we cannot easily deny an ethical relationship to the living and nonliving beings that Western thought and science historically have relegated to this other world. Not only is our own survival dependent upon understanding this sense of dynamic continuity, but—whether that is true or not—the integrity of life for those "others" deserves as much respect and attention as we would reserve for human lives. For Bakunin, it is "the infinite totality of the ceaseless transformations of all existing things" that makes this so.

What exactly do we mean by this transformational, generative force? What is it that drives this infinitely creative process? I want to take a few moments to try to articulate a dynamic that I believe is the key to linking together what Bakunin defines as the generative force in nature and what I believe to be at the heart of all pedagogical relations. It is the key, I think, to a passage between Earth, ethics, and education. To make this passage, I look again to the work of French philosopher Gilles Deleuze, in particular to his development of the dynamic effects within repetitious cycles that he presents as a forceful critique of both Western philosophic traditions and positivist science.

In his groundbreaking work, *Difference and Repetition* (1994), Deleuze presents a powerful critique of paradigms of thought that assert the representation of an orderly world within hierarchized taxonomies and that privilege the Platonic idea of Sameness and Identity that underlie attempts to get to one final truth. Pulling apart established, taken-for-granted ways of thinking that categorize life forms and therefore present them in static groupings or orderly cycles, he urges us toward a sense of beauty and awe in the intensity and chaos generated by forces of differentiation. All life forms reproduce by and through a process of differentiation. As I am reminded by students who study biological science, we are products of an infinitely variable genetic, as well as sociocultural and historical, dance. What I want to try to make clear by delving into Deleuze's thought again is that it is the intensive generative force of difference that paradoxically connects human lives in creativity and change with the "universal" life forces defined by Bakunin as "nature."

For Deleuze, this affirmative life- (and death-) generating force is produced through the movement of "pure difference" pulsating within the spaces provided by every possible relation, human or nonhuman, and in every repetition—social, biological, or geological. The differences internal to all these relational processes of repetition bring forth infinite variation and possibility.

> Even in nature, isochronic rotations are only the outward appearance of a more profound movement, the revolving cycles are only abstractions: placed together, they reveal evolutionary cycles or spirals whose principle is a variable curve, and the trajectory of which has two dissymmetrical aspects, as though it had a right and a left. *It is always in this gap, which should not be confused with the negative, that creatures weave their repetition and receive at the same time the gift of living and dying.*" (Deleuze, 1994, p. 21; emphasis added)

Comparable to Jacques Derrida's concept of the supplemental dynamic at work in any text resulting from the act of reading or interpretation, this "more profound movement" is the result of differences distributed within unlimited space (which may or may not be social), producing unpredictable nomadic variations. Quite apart from Derrida, Deleuze understands this movement to be at work in the natural world as well as the social, movement that will always come to undermine positivism's neat categories, taxonomies, and Plato's divine representations.

Thus describing the moving force behind Bakunin's "ceaseless transformations of all existing things," Deleuze points to "displacements, quickenings, slowdowns, variants or differences which are ultimately capable of leading us far away from the point of departure" (1994, p. 25). He goes on to say,

> such a distribution is demonic rather than divine since it is a peculiarity of demons to leap over the barriers of enclosures, thereby confounding the boundaries between properties. The leap here bears witness to the unsettling difficulties that nomadic distributions introduce into the sedentary structures of representation. (p. 37)

While science looks for sameness, generalities, and commensurability, Deleuze points to singular unpredictable intensities that result from the spaces between living things, ideas, words. Every idea or concept when repeated (by a student, for example) produces something new or different (a slightly different interpretation than perhaps the teacher expected, for example) precisely because there is a singular differential force in operation. That which we have come to call evolution (and which nontraditional scientists like Stephen J. Gould, for example, describe as arbitrary rather than teleological development) is the result of this same ongoing production and distribution of difference within the repetitious cycles of reproduction.

This differential force generates the movement of creativity in ideas, in evolution, in emotion. Most importantly, this intensity does not remain isolated in either the natural world or in our interpretations or social relations; it is the motor force in both.

> Cyclical generalities in nature are the masks of a singularity which appears through their interferences; and beneath the generalities of habit in moral life we rediscover singular processes of learning. The domain of laws must be understood, but always on the basis of a Nature and a Spirit superior to their own laws, which weave their repetition in the depths of the earth and of the heart, where laws do not yet exist. (Deleuze, 1994, p. 25)

The very possibility of evolution in nature or education in human life is generated within this intensive process of repetition and difference.

The continuity that Bakunin seeks with his concept of universal solidarity unfolds paradoxically in Deleuze's work through the force of pure difference, "pure movement, creative of a dynamic space and time." And this is where my awe resides. I feel it rush up my throat or tingle the back of my neck as a flash of excitement signifying that we humans in all our social and cultural relationships are part of a larger, more general, dynamic, changing life force. This is a force holding within it infinite singular possibilities; but it is also finite, capable of being destroyed, as witness the damage done to our woodlands, streams and lakes, the ozone layer, and species after species of wildlife. This dynamic force requires from us a specific kind of attention and respect. And teachers must take up this challenge.

There is a politics and an ethics involved here, as Bakunin and Deleuze both insist. For Deleuze, the generative force created through repetition and difference is *indifferent*, although the ways that we attend to the difference is not. That is, it is not enough to recognize the ways that these variable singularities move and shift boundaries. It is not enough to acknowledge difference, we must also attend ethically to those we would define as "other." In particular, we must face the suffering of the other, created within this life- and death-giving dynamic. As I have argued throughout this book, this relationship between ethics and difference is exactly where education circulates.

Bakunin asserts a clear connection between a universal life force and ethical and political action. To him the ability to intervene and act on behalf of the other's well-being is not a humanly imposed attitude or behavior, but rather part of what is needed for the survival of this complex system:

> In Nature as in Human society which is nothing but Nature, everything that lives does so only under the supreme condition of intervening in the most positive manner in the life of others—intervening in as powerful a manner as the particular nature of a given individual permits it to do so. To do away with this reciprocal influence would spell death in the full sense of the word. (Bakunin, 1953, p. 264)

Awakening to Education

All life depends upon the intervention in and ethical attention to the lives of others, whether they be human or not. Attention to the other, to alterity, to the beautiful generative force of difference, while understanding our interbeing, is the creator of eco-erosic love. We are given joy and awe and life when we attend. Little Tree learned this; my mother taught me this. I write now as a means of awakening educators to it.

While we have begun to take up the critical issue of social justice and multicultural education, the even more fundamental and certainly interwoven question of education's significance to our earthly survival has been left largely untouched by teacher educators. It's time to attend to the Earth as we care for each other. In the wise and passionate words of Michel Serres:

> We used to know how to love our neighbors sometimes, and often the land; we have learned with difficulty to love humanity, which was once so abstract, but which we are starting to encounter more frequently; now we must learn and teach around us the love of the world, or of our Earth, which we can henceforth contemplate as whole. Love our two fathers, natural and human, the land and the neighbor; love humanity, our human mother and our natural mother, the Earth. (1995c, p. 49)

In our relations with our students, in what we ask that they consider, and in their interpretations of these issues and questions lie unforeseeable possibilities for this world, many more than we can know or predict. We must be prepared to attend to these different responses and to encourage an ethical shaping of their potentials for loving our Earth, our local landscapes and neighbors, and those for whom we may believe we have no affinity.

Love and suffering is in the differences, and becoming educated requires careful attention to each of these. I thank my mother for all she's taught me, for the eco-erosic love that she embraced me with to urge me down this educational path. Difficult as it is, it is also the most joyous and beautiful passage in the world.

References

Abram, D. (1996). *The spell of the sensuous*. New York: Vintage.

Alschuler, A. (1980). *School discipline: A socially literate solution*. New York: McGraw Hill.

Althusser, L. (1971). *Lenin and philosophy and other essays*. London: New Left Books.

Anyon, J. (1981). Elementary schooling and distinctions of social class. *Interchange, 12*(2/3), 259-288.

Bakunin, M. (1953). *The political philosophy of Bakunin: Scientific anarchism* (G. P. Maximoff, Ed.). Glencoe, IL: The Free Press.

Barry, L. (1992). *My perfect life*. New York: HarperCollins

Bartky, S. L. (1996). The pedagogy of shame. In C. Luke (Ed.), *Feminisms and pedagogies of everyday life* (pp. 225-241). Albany: State University of New York Press.

Benjamin, A. (1992). Translating origins: Psychoanalysis and philosophy. In L. Venuti (Ed.), *Rethinking translation: Discourse, subjectivity, ideology* (pp. 18-41). London: Routledge.

Benjamin, J. (1988). *The bonds of love*. New York: Pantheon.

Benjamin, W. (1992). The task of the translator. In R. Schulte, & J. Biguenet (Eds.), *Theories of translation: An anthology of essays from Dryden to Derrida* (pp. 71-92). Chicago: University of Chicago Press.

Bordo, S. (1996). Hunger as ideology. In C. Luke (Ed.), *Feminisms and pedagogies of everyday life* (pp. 119-146). Albany: State University of New York Press.

Bowers, C. A. (1984). *The promise of theory: Education and the politics of cultural change*. New York: Longman.

Bowers, C. A. (1993). *Education, cultural myths and the ecological crisis: Toward deep changes*. Albany: State University of New York Press.

Bowers, C. A. (1997). *The culture of denial: Why the environmental movement needs a strategy for reforming universities and public schools*. Albany: State University of New York Press.

Brenkman, J. (1993). *Straight male modern: A cultural critique of psychoanalysis*. New York: Routledge.

Brod, H., & Kaufman, M. (Eds.) (1994). *Theorizing masculinities*. Thousand Oaks, CA: Sage.

Brown, L. M., & Gilligan, C. (1992). *Meeting at the Crossroads: Women's psychology and girls' development*. Cambridge, MA: Harvard University Press.

Capra, F. (1982). *The turning point*. New York: Anchor Books.

Capra, F. (1996). *The web of life: A new scientific understanding of living systems.* New York: Anchor Books.

Carter, F. (1976). *The education of Little Tree.* Albuquerque: University of New Mexico Press.

Chodorow, N. (1978). *The reproduction of mothering: Psychoanalysis and the sociology of gender.* Berkeley: Univesity of California Press.

Chödrön, P. (1997). *When things fall apart: Heart advice for difficult times.* Boston: Shambhala.

Cixous, H. (1981). The Laugh of the Medusa. In E. Marks & I. DeCourtivron (Eds.), *New French feminisms* (pp. 245-264). New York: Schoken Books.

Coates, P. (1998). *Nature: Western attitudes since ancient times.* Berkeley: University of California Press.

Connell, R. W. (1987). *Gender and power.* Cambridge, UK: Polity Press.

Connell, R. W. (1992). A very straight gay: Masculinity, homosexual experience and the dynamics of gender. *American Sociological Review, 57*(6), 735-751.

Cornell, D. (1993). *Transformations: Recollective imagination and sexual difference.* New York: Routledge.

Daignault, J. (1983, October). *Analogies in education: An archaeology without subsoil.* Paper presented at the Conference on Curriculum Theorizing and Classroom Practice, Dayton, OH.

Daignault, J. (1986, October). *Semiotics of educational expression.* Paper presented at the Conference on Curriculum Theory and Classroom Practice, Dayton, OH.

Daignault, J. (1989, October). Curriculum as composition: Who is the composer? Paper presented at the Conference on Curriculum Theorizing and Classroom Practice, Dayton, OH.

Deleuze, G. (1983). *Nietzsche and philosophy* (H. Tomlinson, Trans.). New York: Columbia University Press. (Original work published 1967)

Deleuze, G. (1990). *The logic of sense* (M. Lester, Trans.; C. V. Boundas, Ed.). New York: Columbia University Press. (Original work published 1969)

Deleuze, G. (1994). *Difference and repetition* (P. Patton, Trans.). New York: Columbia University Press. (Original work published 1968)

Deleuze, G., & Guattari, F. (1987). *A thousand plateaus* (B. Massumi, Trans.). Minneapolis: University of Minnesota. (Original work published 1980)

Deleuze, G. & Parnet, C. (1987). *Dialogues* (H. Tomlinson & B. Habberjam, Trans.). New York: Columbia University Press. (Original work published 1977)

Derrida, J. (1979). Living on. In H. Bloom et al. (Eds.), *Deconstruction and criticism* (pp. 75-176). New York: Seabury Press.

Derrida, J. (1985a). Des tours des Babel. In J. F. Graham (Ed.), *Difference in translation* (pp. 165-208). Ithaca, NY: Cornell University Press.

Derrida, J. (1985b). *The ear of the other* (C. McDonald, Ed.; P. Kamuf, Trans.). Lincoln: University of Nebraska Press. (Original work published 1982)

Descombes, V. (1980). *Modern French philosophy.* London: Cambridge University Press.

Dewey, J. (1960). *On Experience, nature and freedom* (R. Bernstein, Ed.). New York: Minton Balch.

Edgerton, S. H. (1996). *Translating the curriculum: Multiculturalism into cultural studies.* New York: Routledge.

Ellsworth, E. (1989). Why doesn't this feel empowering?: Working through the repressive myths of critical pedagogy. *Harvard Educational Review, 59*(3), 297–324.

Foucault, M. (1977). Theatrum philosophicum. In D. F. Bouchard (Ed.), & D. F. Bouchard & S. Simon (Trans.), *Language, counter-memory, practice* (pp. 165–196). Ithaca, NY: Cornell University Press.

Foucault, M. (1980). *The history of sexuality: Vol. 1. An Introduction* (R. Hurley, Trans.). New York: Vintage Books.

Foucault, M. (1989). An ethics of pleasure. In S. Lotringer (Ed.), & J. Johnson (Trans.), *Foucault live: Interviews, 1966–84* (pp. 257–274). New York: Semiotext.

Fraser, N. (1997). *Justice interruptus: Critical reflections on the "postsocialist" condition.* New York: Routledge.

Gilligan, C. (1982). *In a different voice: Psychological theory and women's development.* Cambridge, MA: Harvard University Press.

Girard, R. (1977). *Violence and the sacred.* Baltimore: Johns Hopkins University Press.

Gordon, H. (1988). Learning to think: Hannah Arendt on education for democracy. *Educational Forum, 53*(1), 49–62.

Gore, J. (1993). *The struggle for pedagogies.* London: Routledge.

Graham, J. F. (Ed.). (1985). *Difference in translation.* Ithaca, NY: Cornell University Press.

Grahame, K. (1987). *The wind in the willows.* London: Chancellor Press.

Greene, M. (1978). *Landscapes of learning.* New York: Teachers College Press.

Greene, M. (1988). *The dialectic of freedom.* New York: Teachers College Press.

Gutterman, D. (1994). Postmodern theories of masculinity. In H. Brod & M. Kaufman (Eds.), *Theorizing masculinity* (pp. 219–238). Thousand Oaks, CA: Sage.

Hanh, Thich Naht. (1988). *The sun my heart.* Berkeley, CA: Parallax Press.

Hanh, Thich Nhat. (1993). *Love in action: Writings on nonviolent social change.* Berkeley, CA: Parallax Press.

Harvey, D. (1996). *Justice, nature and the geography of difference.* Oxford, UK: Blackwell.

Heidegger, M. (1962). *Being and time* (J. Macquarrie & E. Robinson, Trans.). San Francisco: Harper and Row.

hooks, b. (1990). *Yearning: Race, gender and cultural politics.* Boston: Southend Press.

hooks, b. (1996). *Teaching to transgress.* Boston: Southend Press.

Irigaray, L. (1985). *This sex which is not one* (C. Porter, Trans.). Ithaca, NY: Cornell University Press.

Johnson, B. (1985). Taking fidelity philosophically. In J. F. Graham (Ed.), *Difference in translation* (pp. 142–148). Ithaca, NY: Cornell University Press.

Kaufman, M. (1993). *Cracking the armour: Power, pain and the lives of men.* Toronto: Viking Books.

Kimmel, M., & Kaufman, M. (1994). Weekend warriors: The new men's movement.

In H. Brod and M. Kaufman (Eds.), *Theorizing masculinity* (pp. 259–288). Thousand Oaks, CA: Sage.

Kliebard, H. (1995). *The struggle for the American curriculum, 1893–1958* (2nd ed.). New York: Routledge.

Lewis, M. (1993). *Without a word: Teaching beyond women's silence.* London: Routledge.

Luke, C. (Ed.). (1996). *Feminisms and pedagogies of everyday life.* Albany: State University of New York Press.

Lyotard, J. F. (1984). *The post-modern condition: A report on knowledge* (G. Bennington & B. Massumi, Trans.). Minneapolis: University of Minnesota Press.

Lyotard, J. F. (1988). *The differend: Phrases in dispute* (G. Van Den Abbeele, Trans.). Minneapolis: University of Minnesota Press.

Mac an Ghaill, M. (1994). *The making of men: Masculinities, sexualities and schooling.* Philadelphia: Open University Press.

Mairs, N. (1994). *Voice lessons: On becoming a (woman) writer.* Boston: Beacon Press.

Martusewicz, R. A. (1988). *The will to reason: An archaeology of womanhood and education, 1880–1920.* Unpublished doctoral dissertation, University of Rochester, Rochester, NY.

McElroy, S. C. (1997). *Animals as teachers and healers: True stories and reflections.* New York: Ballantine Books.

McKibben, B. (1995). *Hope, human and wild: True stories of living lightly on the earth.* Boston: Little, Brown.

Mehuron, K., & Percesepe, G. (Eds.). (1995). *Free spirits: Feminist philosophers on culture.* Englewood Cliffs, NJ: Prentice Hall.

Middleton, S. (1993). *Educating feminists.* New York: Teachers College Press.

Neuman, A., & Peterson, P. L. (1997). *Learning from our lives: Women, research and autobiography in education.* New York: Teachers College Press.

Nussbaum, M. C. (1990). *Love's knowledge: Essays on philosophy and literature.* New York: Oxford University Press.

Orenstein, P. (1994). *School girls: Young women, self-esteem, and the confidence gap.* New York: Anchor Books.

Ortega y Gasset, J. (1992). The misery and the splendor of translation. In R. Schulte & J. Biguenet (Eds.), *Theories of translation: An anthology of essays from Dryden to Derrida* (pp. 93–112). Chicago: The University of Chicago Press.

Pagano, J. (1990). *Exiles and communities: Teaching in the patriarchal wilderness.* Albany: State University of New York Press.

Pinar, W. F. (1994). *Autobiography, politics and sexuality: Essays in curriculum theory, 1972–1992.* New York: Peter Lang.

Pinar, W. F., & Grumet, M. (1976). *Toward a poor curriculum.* Dubuque, IA: Kendall/Hunt.

Pipher, M. B. (1994). *Reviving Ophelia: Saving the selves of adolescent girls.* New York: Putnam.

Plumwood, V. (1993). *Feminism and the mastery of nature.* London: Routledge.

Quint, S. (1994). *Schooling homeless children: A working model for America's public schools.* New York: Teachers College Press.

Rich, A. (1983). Compulsory heterosexuality and lesbian existence. In A. Snitow, C. Stansell, & S. Thompson (Eds.), *Powers of desire: The politics of sexuality*. New York: Monthly Review Press.

Roife, A. (1993). *If you knew me*. New York: Warner Books.

Ryan, W. (1976). *Blaming the victim*. New York: Vintage.

Schulte, R., & Biguenet, J. (Eds.). (1992). *Theories of translation: An anthology of essays from Dryden to Derrida*. Chicago: University of Chicago Press.

Sennett, R., & Cobb, J. (1972). *The hidden injuries of class*. New York: Vintage Books.

Serres, M. (1982). Hermes: Literature, science, philosophy (J. V. Harari & D. F. Bell, Trans.). Baltimore: Johns Hopkins Univesity Press. (Original work published 1968)

Serres, M. (1989). *Detachment* (G. James & R. Federman, Trans.). Athens: Ohio University Press. (Original work published 1983)

Serres, M. (1991). *Rome: The book of foundations* (F. McCarren, Trans.). Palo Alto, CA: Stanford University Press. (Original work published 1983)

Serres, M. (with Latour, B.). (1995a). *Conversations on science, culture and time* (R. Lapidus, Trans.). Ann Arbor: University of Michigan Press.

Serres, M. (1995b). *Genesis* (G. James & J. Nielson, Trans.). Ann Arbor: University of Michigan Press. (Original work published 1982)

Serres, M. (1995c). *The natural contract* (E. MacArthur & W. Paulson, Trans.). Ann Arbor: University of Michigan Press. (Original work published 1990)

Serres, M. (1997). *The troubadour of knowledge* (S. F. Glazer with W. Paulson, Trans.). Ann Arbor: University of Michigan Press. (Original work published 1991)

Singer, P. (1993). *Practical ethics* (2nd ed.). Cambridge, UK: Cambridge University Press.

Singer, P. (1995). *How are we to live? Ethics in an age of self-interest*. Amherst, NY: Prometheus Books.

Smith, G. A., & Williams, D. R. (Eds.). (1998). *Ecological education in action: On weaving education, culture and the environment*. Albany: State University of New York Press.

Spring, J. (2000). *The intersection of cultures: Multicultural education in the United States and the global economy* (2nd ed.). Boston: McGraw Hill.

Starhawk. (1995). Power, authority, and mystery: Ecofeminism and earth-based spirituality. In K. Mehuron & G. Percesepe (Eds.), *Free spirits: Feminist philosophers on culture* (pp. 274–283). Englewood Cliffs, NJ: Prentice Hall.

Tall, D. (1993). *From where we stand: Recovering a sense of place*. New York: Knopf.

Tanenbaum, L. (1999). *Slut!: Growing up female with a bad reputation*. New York: Seven Stories Press.

Taylor, J., Gilligan, C., & Sullivan, A. M. (1995). *Between voice and silence: Women and girls, race and relationship*. Cambridge, MA: Harvard University Press.

Tuan, Y.-F. (1977). *Space and place: The perspective of experience*. Minneapolis: University of Minnesota Press.

Venuti, L. (Ed.). (1992). *Rethinking translation: Discourse, subjectivity, ideology*. London: Routledge.

Walkerdine, V. (1992). *Schoolgirl fictions*. London: Verso.

Weeks, J. (1989). *Sexuality and its discontents: Meanings, myths, and modern sexualities.* London: Routledge.

Weil, S. (1951). *Waiting for God.* New York: Harper and Row.

Weil, S. (1956). *The notebooks of Simone Weil* (Arthur Wells, Trans.). New York: G. P. Putnams Sons.

Weil, S. (1972). *Gravity and grace.* London: Routledge.

Weil, S. (1979). *Lectures on philosophy.* Cambridge, UK: Cambridge University Press.

Weiler, K. (1988). *Women teaching for change.* New York: Bergin and Garvey.

Weis, L. (1995). Identity formation and the process of "othering": Unraveling sexual threads. *Educational Foundations, 9*(1), 17–33.

West, C. (1994). *Race matters.* New York: Vintage Books.

Young-Eisendrath, P. (1996). *The gifts of suffering: Finding insight, compassion and renewal.* Reading, MA: Addison-Wesley.

Index

About the Author

Rebecca A. Martusewicz is a professor in the Department of Teacher Education and the Women's Studies Program at Eastern Michigan University. Rebecca sees her primary work to be preparing practicing and prospective teachers to deal with and create practices around the problem of social justice. She is editor with William Reynolds of *Inside/Out: Contemporary Critical Perspectives in Education* (1994) as well as several book chapters and journal articles dealing with post-structuralism, feminism, and education. She is also editor of *Educational Studies, Journal of the American Education Studies Association.*